Mia Walsch is an author from Melbourne, Australia. She studied Creative Writing at the University of Wollongong and has previously published three novels, the first of which won a Victorian Premier's Literary Award. This is her first non-fiction book.

# MONEY FOR SOMETHING

## The memoir of a sex worker

# MIA WALSCH

JOHN BLAKE

Published by John Blake Publishing,
80–1 Wimpole Street,
Marylebone
London W1G 9RE

www.facebook.com/johnblakebooks 
twitter.com/jblakebooks 

First published in paperback in 2020

Paperback ISBN: 978-1-78946-335-4
Ebook ISBN: 978-1-78946-349-1

British Library Cataloguing-in-Publication Data:

A catalogue record for this book is available from the British Library.

Original cover design by Alissa Dinallo, adapted by www.envydesign.co.uk

Printed and bound in Great Britain by Clays Ltd, Elcograf S.p.A.

1 3 5 7 9 10 8 6 4 2

Every reasonable effort has been made to trace copyright-holders of material
reproduced in this book, but if any have been inadvertently overlooked the publish-
ers would be glad to hear from them.

John Blake Publishing is an imprint of Bonnier Books UK
www.bonnierbooks.co.uk

*For all the exquisite, complex and wonderful
women I met along the way . . .*

*All names have been changed, even the fake ones.*

Content Warning: Suicide attempt, self-harm, drug use, injecting drug use. Please use this information to keep yourself safe.

When I was a teenager I covered my school folders and diaries with the 'adult services' pages from the newspaper. Then I'd take a magazine and snip out images of rock stars and strange or funny headlines and layer them over the top, arranging and rearranging till they were perfect. The glue-stick made my fingers tacky, picking up grubby newsprint from the paper and smearing it around as I pressed the pictures down. The black-and-white words and dot-matrix images of the ads peeked out, stark against the bright cuttings atop. I'd cover the whole thing in clear, self-adhesive plastic, pushing out all the bubbles just so, sealing in the newspaper ink for all time.

I didn't know then that I'd later spend three years working my way through a good number of the establishments advertised there.

Or maybe I did. I don't know.

I was a fucking weird kid.

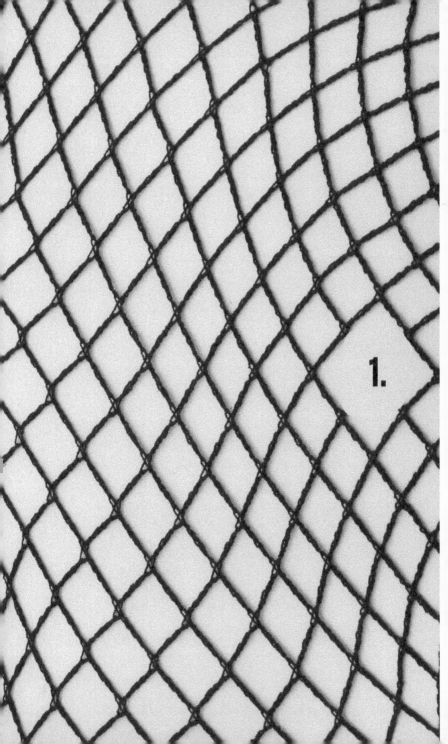

'We're going to have to let you go.'

Alison doesn't look mad, she looks worried. Which is somehow worse. I sit hunched across from her, pulling at my sleeves and trying to look everywhere except at her kind, concerned face.

'Yes, that's okay. I understand.'

Alison's office doesn't have a window and it makes me feel like I'm suffocating. How can she stand this? It's a bit like the filing room, where I've spent my days these past few months, rows of laden shelves hanging above me. I keep waiting for them to collapse and bury me. After some speed-fuelled sleepless nights, I swear I'd seen them teeter, curve and bend. I was excited for it to happen, to disappear beneath a mound of manila folders, suffocate under reams of paper. I couldn't fucking wait.

But now Alison from HR is firing me, so it's never going to happen.

She's got pictures of her kids pinned up on the walls, sunshine-blond children laughing from glossy photographs. I pull my vision back and focus on her highlighted hair, a rainbow of carefully dyed ambers and caramels.

Alison is too nice. She shouldn't have to put up with my shit. I deserve to be fired. I'm surprised it hasn't happened already.

I mean, how many days can I call in sick before they get jack of it? Especially when I'm not actually sick, I'm more often recovering from drug binges. Or actually just on drugs. Or I'm sobbing on the floor for no reason, unable to get up. Or I'm recovering from some stupid fucking half-hearted suicide attempt with bandages on my stupid fucking wrists. That's not sick, that's irresponsible and out of control. And even if I could show up on time, or at all, they don't want girls like me working at insurance companies. Their file clerks should be more normal. You know, with layered hair and corporate casual wardrobes and their sights on careers. Not strange girls like me. I've got messy, dyed-black hair that I cut myself (terribly), and most of my clothes come out of a second-hand bin and cost four dollars. I have no plans for the future; I live in a constant whirlwind present, like an animal. People at work like me, I think. But I stick out. I do not belong.

Anyway, they've had enough. It's okay, I was pretty sure

this was going to happen. It's actually a relief. Pretending to be normal for eight hours every day was sucking at my soul. I managed it for about two months before the cracks started to show.

Alison shakes my hand and the bandage on my wrist pops out of my sleeve a little, so we both pretend not to see it, and she walks me to the elevator.

'Take care of yourself, Mia,' she says, and she means it, but I'm not going to. The elevator pings, opens, and I get in. I don't turn around until the doors have closed. I don't want to see her worried face.

When I get home, I undress, cry, punch a few bongs, stare at the cracked ceiling in my room. My window is wound all around with ivy, which turns the light that spills in green. I watch shadows play across my sick-hued skin for a while. I'm preparing myself.

For a while now I've had this cutting in my handbag. A little scrap of newspaper like the ones I used to rub all over with a glue-stick, slap down on my schoolbooks and my friends would all giggle at the audacity of it.

I'm not scared. I'm not anything. It just makes sense. Of course I'm going to call. I was always going to call. I take the slip of grey paper out and dial the number. They ask me if I want to interview that day. Why yes, I do.

The cutting says: 'Erotic Massage. Good money. No sex.'

\* \* \*

It's the new millennium. I've just turned nineteen. I'm skinny and dark-haired and braless, tripping down terrace-lined backstreets towards the station and my sex work destiny in a terrible outfit. I've got so many, but imagine, maybe, a black halter top that's really just a scrap of fabric, and a tiny miniskirt along with battered Mary Janes.

I'm in Newtown, the land of my dreams. To get here, I left home with fifty bucks and a bag, stayed with a friend for a week, then posed nude for a men's magazine to get enough cash for a bond. I got a job at an insurance company doing admin, but yeah, you remember how that went?

Now I'm clack-clacking down the street to Redfern Station in my Mary Janes, leaving behind a neat little room full of kerbside-collection furniture, all mine for the grand sum of eighty dollars a week. I've got as much pot as I can smoke, not enough to kill every single feeling I have, but enough to try.

I am living the dream.

And I'll do whatever it takes to keep the dream alive.

A nondescript door on a main street on the lower North Shore opens to reveal a dim stairway. I stumble-trip up and am greeted at the top by a heavily made-up blonde in a great deal of leopard print.

'Hi, I'm Iris! Are you Mia?'

I nod, still blinking, trying to adjust to the soft-lit halls after scrambling through the bright sunlight outside. She walks me down a hallway punctuated with doors. Doors everywhere, all closed. Behind those doors must be where this 'good money' is earned, with 'no sex'. If not sex, then what? Surely dudes don't often part with the kind of money one would describe as 'good' without getting at least a little action. Iris is blabbering away as we walk, talking about doubles and day shifts, but I'm barely listening. I'm too distracted by the doors. Is real live erotic massage happening right now?

Finally, we reach the last door. A tall gorgeous woman leans against the jamb.

'Hi Mia, I'm Serena.' I shake her hand. It is soft, and later I will learn those soft hands are the culmination of many years spent coated in slick massage oil. Serena has nice nails, perfect hair. She has nice everything, really. She leads me into a tiny office, and we sit down at the desk. There is no natural light in her office – the window is completely blacked out. It could be any time outside. Or no time.

'So, how old are you?' Serena says.

'Nineteen.'

'Great! I'll tell you a little bit about the business. Here at Slide, we offer a fully nude erotic massage service with body-to-body contact and hand relief.'

Hand relief?

What on earth is that?

Hand-jobs? No sex, but yes, hand-jobs? That's not so bad.

9

I mull it over a little and reason that it's not as gross as having my hands immersed in filthy dishwater for eight hours, which is what many of my previous jobs entailed. She goes over the house rules (what on earth does 'no extras' mean?), hours (the late shift runs until 2 am), the prices and my cut, which is 50 per cent. It seems a bit of a rip-off seeing as the dicks will be in my hands, but I reason that they do solicit the penises towards my hands and also provide a private space for all this dick-grabbing to occur, trusting that there are actually rooms behind all the doors. I nod and smile.

'You've got a great look,' Serena says. 'You'll do really well here.' I think I know what she means. I'm nineteen, but I look about fifteen. I'm tiny, I barely ever eat solids that aren't ecstasy pills, so my baby fat has melted away. My hair is nice and shiny, and my mental illness is masked by my pretty smile. Even if it wasn't, it doesn't really matter.

'When do you want to start? Tonight?'

'Um, how about tomorrow?'

I need time to prepare.

I assume that men only want to pay lots of money to have their backs rubbed and their cocks pulled by what I think of as 'real, proper girls' who appear to actually care what they look like. I can do an okay job of pretending, but I'm not a real 'proper girl'. I don't own a single smudge of makeup or any matching lingerie. All of my undies are ragged Bonds bikini briefs and I haven't worn a bra for months, since my boobs shrank along with the rest of me when I stopped eating. My clothes are wacky ensembles that I've collected from various op shops in Sydney's inner west. I need time to craft a more fitting persona for the kind of person who trades sexual favours for money.

'Great! Thursday nights are always busy. While you're here, did you want to come and meet the girls?'

No.

No, I really don't want to meet the girls, but I pretend that I do. I have this obscure terror of large groups of women, especially beautiful ones. It's a fear mixed with awe and a little bit of lust. I'm always afraid that I might give myself away as some kind of imposter woman who also might want to kiss them and maybe feel their boobs. Because I do.

Serena leads me across the hall to another small room, a windowless box with doors on each side. It's crammed with a futon sofa and looks like a femme-bomb went off inside. Lingerie, makeup and shoes are *everywhere*, with paths beaten through the refuse. I toe a discarded bottle of foundation out from underneath my foot. Sprawled across the sofa are four incredibly bored-looking women in their underwear. They are watching music videos on the TV opposite and they glance up at me.

'This is the new girl! She doesn't have a name yet. She's starting tomorrow, so, Sandy, you can help show her the ropes.' A blonde woman in a purple teddy nods dully, her long, tanned limbs spilling out of lace, arranged haphazardly on the lumpy futon. I can't tell if this non-reaction is good or bad. At least no one is looking at me, which lowers the chance that they are judging me, or seeing me for what I really am.

Serena walks me to the door and tells me I need to pick a name. I'm too shell-shocked to make any decisions right now, and the name thing seems important. She gives me her mobile number and tells me to text her my name later that night. They need to start advertising the new masseuse. Advertise? Me? Why would anyone want to do that? I don't even know what I'm doing.

A new name is like a second chance, the opportunity to be all the things I haven't been able to be. Of course, I'm drawing a complete blank.

'What's a sexy name?' I ask my boyfriend.

'Jesus, I don't know,' he says, not looking up from his computer.

'What says "Pay me money to touch your penis"?'

'Sharon.'

'Come on! Help me!'

'Sheila,' he says, pushing away his keyboard and poking me in the ribs.

'No!'

We go back and forth for a while, finally settling on Sasha. It will do.

He thinks this whole 'sex work' thing is a bit of a laugh. He's a lot older than me. He was my flatmate, but we started sleeping together right after I moved in. I have a terrible habit of doing things like that.

Our relationship involves smoking a great deal of marijuana, doing handfuls of other drugs whenever we can afford them (also when we can't) and sleeping with as many other people as we can, often together. He's a musician. Of course he is. He's also a waiter. He's really fucking smart and teaches me a lot of things. He's also a complete arse. That's okay, I'm a psycho bitch. We work pretty well together.

He will do.

His name is Leo. I simultaneously hate and love him. It's my first relationship out of high school.

With the last of my corporate job money, I buy a new bra, some nice undies, and a sheer, black form-fitting negligee thing. Before my shift, I wander into the pharmacy and peer at the makeup shelves. Fuck, I don't know! I pick a foundation and powder at random, then some mascara (the pink and green tube, that's what I see everyone use), a little case of eye shadow and some light pink lip gloss. I'm sweaty and confused as I walk up the stairs, half an hour early. A different receptionist lets me in, a small Asian woman with a boyish figure and pixie haircut. Her name is Suzy and when she opens the door to the staff lounge to usher me in everyone looks up.

'Um, hi. I'm Sasha. I'm new.'

They mob me.

'It's really nice to meet you!'

'Is this your first shift?'

'Have you worked before?'

I am overwhelmed but relieved that the pack seems to have already accepted me as one of their own. 'No, I've never done this before.'

'Oh, she's a virgin! Don't worry, we'll show you what to do. You'll do really well here, guys like that fresh look.' This is industry slang for 'old perves love teenage girls'. It's my niche; everyone has one.

'How old are you?'

'Nineteen.'

'Oh, tell them you're eighteen, they will love that.'

'Uh, okay, I will then.'

More women are filling the room. It's changeover, so the day shift is still in, getting dressed slowly and catching up with the night shift. Everyone is in varying states of disarray and undress and I'm not sure where to look. Boobs! Boobs all over the place! Big ones, small ones, puffy nipples, inverted nipples, slightly lopsided, perfectly surgically sculpted. I love them all.

As I ponder over all the fine tits on display, a woman sticks her head around the corner.

'Hi, I'm Vee.' Vee has one of the thickest New Zealand accents I've ever heard. 'Uv gut a cliunt cumming un tun munutes, do ya wunna come un wuth me?'

I am baffled, but gradually come to realise that she is asking me to join her in a booking so I can get an idea of what I'm supposed to do.

'Sure, thanks. I'll just be a minute!'

There's a small room off to the side lined with lit mirrors. I take a seat there and begin to smear my face inexpertly with foundation. I have no idea what I'm doing – the last time I applied my own makeup was at my high school formal and I made a hell of a mess of it then too. Once I've done all the makeup parts I believe I'm supposed to do (foundation, powder, eye shadow, lips, mascara? That sounds right, yeah?) I put on my special fancy knickers, slip into the negligee and strap a pair of velvet platforms on my feet (the last time I wore these was to my school formal too). I'm sure in daylight I'd look a complete mess, but in the dim, soft-lit dressing room, I'm an exquisite creature. With my sleek dark hair, sexy get-up and shimmery pink lips I look incredibly female. I look … beautiful. Can I say that? Am I allowed to think I look beautiful?

I spent a long while in high school getting called a fuckin' dog.

I had acne, weird haircuts and gross clothes. I *did* have big boobs, but I was also chunky, not in a specifically overweight way, but more in this awkward, just a bit-too-big-for-my-features kind of way. Others saw me as unattractive, and so did I. There was a calm acceptance of the fact: I am not a pretty girl. I am ugly.

I changed physically over the years and started to look like I do now, which I believe I can get away with calling 'pretty cute'. But even though my looks had changed, my opinion of myself didn't, not for a very long time. It's funny how that works.

I don't really know what I see in the mirror any more. Maybe because I'm really seeing something else. I look like a picture of someone, or a doll. People will tell me this over and over in those first years, that I'm a doll. That I'm so small and bendable. I feel like a doll too. As if I'm made of plastic. Like I've got a PVC coating over my limbs. I've felt like this for a long time. As though nothing is real – not myself, and especially no one else. So, it doesn't matter, really, what I do.

It's why I can do this without a second thought. Yes, lose my job. Yes, drugs and no food and a much older boyfriend and a relationship that's dysfunctional to say the least. Why not interview at a massage parlour? Yes, follow a blowsy Kiwi chick down the hallway to engage in sexual acts for money for the very first time, without any fear. People have always called me brave, and I'll grow more into that reputation, but not for a while yet. At this point it's not bravery at all. It's that nothing feels real, so nothing matters. It's easy to do things – huge things, good things, bad things or things that fall along a line in between – when nothing matters.

The room is dim, light glowing softly from above. The dude is already there, lying facedown on the table, draped with a towel. His bare back glimmers with droplets of water from the shower. Vee's voice drops an octave when she talks in here. I stand awkwardly at the head of the table and watch as Vee slips the ties of her bikini top down. I drink up the way her strong hands ply his thick-muscled back. He gives me a smile before sighing, his eyes rolling back a little before they close. He looks really ... content. Happy and peaceful.

Vee breathes softly against him, whispers in his ear, brings her body close and undulates over him. His hand snakes out and pulls the ties at the sides of her bikini bottoms. She helps him drag them down and his hand cups her bare arse. The dimpled flesh I saw there as we smoked in the brighty lit kitchen beforehand is smoothed in the soft light. She works her body over his, murmuring things I can't hear. She looks to me and mouths, 'Your turn.' I slip my clothes off, both of their eyes on me. When I slide my fancy panties down, they get stuck on the buckle of my shoes. Fuck. *Fuck!* Finally, I kick them away. The room smells like grapeseed oil and, under that, sweat. His back is slick with oil and water but is smooth and cool. My hands glide up the straps of muscle along his spine and he exhales, relaxing again. My body follows my hands and I work myself against him.

'I've never done this before,' I say, pressing my breasts into his side.

'You're doing a great job.'

After a while we flip him over and there's his cock, hard and thrusting upwards. It surprises me, I kind of forgot it would be there. Vee avoids it carefully, working around it, moving closer, bit by bit. He's got a hand on each of our arses. I trust his hand there, and he doesn't try to grab me anywhere else. I can barely feel it anyway. Vee starts to tease his cock and I watch it lengthen in her hands. She grabs my hand and, with both our hands stroking him in rhythm, soon he's panting. Vee aims with an experienced hand and he comes onto his own belly, white goo pooling in his bellybutton.

And that's it.

I don't know why I expect to feel different, but I don't. Not a scrap. It's like losing my virginity. It seems like it will be this huge deal, but it's not. I had no idea how I might feel afterwards, but I certainly wasn't expecting this. I was scared I might feel bad, or guilty or disgusted. I don't. I really don't feel much of anything ... Pleased? A little charged up? Also, weirdly turned on, but not by this pale, bulky, perfectly nice forty-ish dude, but by myself. Like I've tapped into this well of something inside me. I knew it was there, I'd tasted traces of it before. It's partly feeling a sick kind of glory in my sexual objectification, but also relishing the way I've harnessed it, flipped it over and used it for my own purposes. Turned it into something tangible.

Cash.


It's one thing to help a seasoned expert with a booking, it's another to go it alone. Ten minutes after I finish the training session with Vee, the doorbell sounds, and I line up with the other women outside the door of the waiting room. One by one they go in and meet the client. When it's my turn, I harness all my bravery and walk in, closing the door awkwardly behind me. I have no idea what I'm supposed to say.

'Um, hello. I'm Sasha. This is my first night.'

'Hi Sasha, I'm Steve,' he says, friendly and familiar, like we're at the post office, or saying hello over the back fence. 'How are you finding it so far?'

'Um, great!'

He looks like a pretty standard guy; like someone I might have worked with at the insurance company. He smells like expensive cologne and new car. I glance around the room, unable to think of anything to say.

'Is there anyone else to meet?' he asks.

'No, I think I'm the last,' I say, backing towards the door. 'I'll go get the receptionist.'

'Nice to meet you,' he says, and I scurry out into reception. How mortifying. I decide I'm awful at this and guess I should just pack up my bags and go home, but then the receptionist, Suzy, comes out of the waiting room and says he's chosen me.

Dear god, why? I'm sure I didn't impress him with my wit.

I'm not scared exactly, I'm just worried about fucking the booking up, not being able to pull his dick right or something. I mean, hand-jobs aren't an intrinsic skill. I put Steve away in the room to shower and head back to the staff lounge.

'You'll be fine!' they tell me as I voice my worries.

'Are you sure?'

'Yeah, it's nothing! Just give him a good time, he won't know the difference.'

I bite at my nails as I go back in. Steve is out of the shower and sitting, towel-wrapped, on the massage table. The suit and wire-rimmed spectacles he was wearing during the intro are placed neatly on the chair at the side of the room. I take a deep breath and try to harness my sexy. I walk over to him, trying to be liquid and luxe in my heels, but feeling clunky and misshapen instead.

'Hi,' he says.

'Hi,' I say, and I'm lost. How do I begin? I guess first thing is first – that towel. I run my fingers down his chest, gently, spider-like, and he sucks in air sharply. I creep down towards the towel, come in close, and as I unwrap him, I whisper softly in his ear.

'You won't be needing this.'

He exhales, his eyes closing, back rounding, relaxing.

I get it. I get it now. I just need to 'act as if'. That's a thing I've heard from a counsellor before.

*Maybe you're not coping or happy or a functional adult. But maybe you act as if you are.*

I need to act like professional sexy bitch. If I can pretend well enough, no one will ever know I'm not.

The booking flows like an oily, dim-lit dream from there. I rub and slip across his back, flip him over, and work myself across his chest. When it comes to the ending, my hand-job is sufficient and produces the desired result.

*I can do this*, I think as I shower afterwards, soaping the oil and the remnants of Steve off my body.

I just need to pretend I'm the sexiest fucking bitch in this place, and maybe one day it will be true.


I spend the rest of the night in and out of the tiny staff lounge, working, chatting and telling stories. I soon learn everyone loves it when someone new starts because it's a fresh opportunity to tell all your best stories. The women seem to like me, to my endless surprise. And I really like them.

The connection is instant, and I haven't felt this close to a bunch of women in a long time. I miss that specific female camaraderie. It's been hard for me to make friends since I moved, not just because I'm new to the city, but because I'm a total nutcase and also addicted to drugs. Here? I'm finding kindred. It's easy to talk to these women, tell them my deepest secrets. Look where we are. What else do we have to hide?

I make a neat stack of cash that night, not a huge pile but enough to maybe pay back a little of the rent money I'd nicked from our communal stash earlier in the week to buy drugs. Of course, I'll keep some of my earnings to buy more drugs. Or shoes. I haven't decided yet.

I catch a taxi home through the night streets and Leo is up when I fumble the lock at 2 am.

'How was it?' he asks.

'Okay. Fun. Weird.' I pull out the stash of cash.

'Profitable, I see.'

'Yeah, not too bad.'

I punch ten or so bongs before I go to bed. It's not as though I'm doing it to cope with the fact that I've just done my first night of sex work. The fact that I made a few guys come for money feels just fine. The ten bongs are pretty normal – I smoke a lot of weed. And anyway, it's okay. I've got money to buy more tomorrow.

'Have you met Zara yet?' Everyone keeps asking me all through my second shift, a day shift. Selling sexual favours in the daytime is a different kettle of fish to lounging about in the parlour deep in the evening. Night-time feels right for sex work, daytime has a different vibe. I peel in at 10 am with a baguette and a huge bottle of OJ, my daily staples, or – the only food I ever actually eat. As I chug juice and smoke in the daylit kitchen, Sandy joins me. She's a regular day girl, a friendly dirty blonde from the North Shore in a lacy pink nightie. I'm crammed into the same outfit as before, quickly washed and dried over the bathtub at home in preparation. I need more clothes.

'Who's Zara? Everyone keeps asking me if I've met her.'

'She's pretty cool and really nice. Everyone likes Zara.'

Vee walks in and lights a cigarette. 'Zara? She's fabulous. She has really amazing hair.'

I don't get to find out why Zara's hair is so amazing

because Iris sticks her head in the door and tells us there's a client to meet in room one.

Guys who come in during the day aren't like the ones who come in at night. They comprise two main groups – retirees and dudes from nearby offices in North Sydney on their lunch breaks. They are businesslike, generally pretty friendly and easier to handle than the night-time fellas, some of whom come in pretty plastered. I hate drunk people. At this stage, I don't drink at all. I save myself and my precious energies for drugs. More on that later.

Anyway, day shift. There's a much more laid-back ambiance. I come in, fresh from the morning and not yet marred by any daily frustrations. I'm relatively clear-headed and about as relaxed as I can get. (Hint: this is actually not very relaxed.)

The day shift women are also a bit of a different breed, less frenetic than those on the night shift. A lot of mums and older women favour the day shift, but also people like me, who aren't interested in having a day job (or can't keep one). Good money can be made on day shift, but it's harder. Nights are … darker. There are a lot of women who work fulltime jobs and bolster their income with wads of extra cash. Night shifts have more of a potential to be a party. Clients are more likely to be drunk or to bring drugs.

Me being me, I never pick a side. I do both day and night shifts. I'm like that.

The way it goes is like this: a guy trips up the stairway, watched by reception and all us workers on little black-and-white CCTV screens. The receptionist puts him in a room, and we traipse in, one by one, to meet him. We each give a little spiel ('Hi, I'm Sasha, I'm new' is enough for me for the moment) and the receptionist pops back in after to find out who he wants to see. Sometimes he doesn't want to see anyone and leaves. This is rarely because he hasn't seen anyone he likes, but more because he's a time-wasting arsehole. I learn quickly that there are men who take pleasure from gawking at and then summarily rejecting sex workers. They see it as a legitimate pastime, a way to keep themselves amused, bolster their ego, and ogle some real live girls in their undies. There are a lot of men like this, far more than you would think (well, far more than I ever thought, because I never imagined such men existed).

If he is legit, the dude makes his choice, pays his way and then is instructed to shower, and shower well. It's important with some to really reiterate the importance of the showering. Even still, many don't do it properly and some even just splash water on their hair and then wait for some strange girl to touch their unclean skin for money.

Men are complex creatures. Either that, or they're very simple. I can't decide.

Meanwhile, the receptionist sticks her head into the girls' room to find us all slumped in front of the television watching something uncomplicated (music videos most often, but sometimes talk shows like Maury Povich or Oprah; all the best parlours have cable).

'Sasha, half an hour in room two.'

Depending on how familiar or cute or weird or creepy or odorous the dude is, or how broke I am, I either punch the air with a whoop, or sigh and head off down the hallway to pretend I'm totally keen on some strange guy for the allotted timeframe and not a second more. The rooms all have clocks right beside the tissues and bottles of grapeseed massage oil, and I make a note of the time when I walk in. I massage him inexpertly then oil myself up, climb aboard and go to town, sliding my naked body over his. After: the customary hand-job. When the deed is done and the paid-for time is spent, he showers, dresses and I see him out the door with air kisses and promises for next time. I shower furiously, clean the room (spray and dry the shower, replace the towels), and head back to the staff lounge, hopefully with some bizarre or raucous anecdote to share.

Rinse and repeat. And repeat. If I'm lucky.

My one-thirty appointment cajoles me into the shower with him.

'Don't wet my hair or my face,' I warn him. 'You might see what I really look like.' He laughs as I soap his back, press my tits against his skin. I've slipped very easily into the false intimacy of the job. My boundaries are all shattered, always have been and I don't know why, so it's simple to become intimate with this transient parade of strange men. The rules of the house serve as my set of boundaries now. It's a firm, fast rule that no one here does 'extras'. From the start, this was pressed to me. The workers gathered around and explained that offering extra services was not only an unfair advantage above the others, but that it was also gross and unnecessary.

'We aren't *prostitutes*,' says a beautiful Lebanese girl called Nissa. Her boyfriend is involved in various illicit things and she says he'd kill her if he found out about her working at the parlour. 'If they want anything else, they could go down the road to Indulge. They give *blow jobs* there.'

The girls all hiss with disgust, as if there's a huge chasm between the jobs of hand and blow. I don't see it, but in the eyes of these women, it's massive. What's so wrong with a blow job? What is the heinous difference between taking a cock into your mouth, over taking it in your hand?

'The clients will ask for extras all the time,' Sandy warns me. 'It gets really fucking old. Like, if you want a gobby, go down the road to Indulge. It's fine there. But they never stop asking, no matter how many times you tell them no.'

'So, Sasha, do you do extras?' the client asks. They told me his name when he chose me in the line-up, but I can't remember it. Steve? So many of them are called Steve.

He says it so casually that it's easy to imagine him asking it regularly. Repeatedly. I pause in my long slide up Maybe-Steve's flabby side, easing my tits away.

'No, I'm sorry. I don't.'

'Never hurts to ask.' He sighs and puts his hands behind his head. I clamber up onto the table and tease his belly slowly with my tits. He sighs. 'That's a shame. I'd pay a hundred bucks to taste your pussy.'

He must note my momentary pause. A hundred bucks? To eat me out? I encourage people to do that for free all the time!

'Sorry, Steve.'

'It's Mark.'

Fuck! The ones that aren't called Steve are almost *always* called Mark.

'Sorry, Mark. It's tempting but I can't. We don't do extras here.'

He laughs. 'Who told you that?'

I sit back between his legs, my body gleaming with oil and hands gripping his meaty, hairy legs. 'Those are the rules!'

'I think you'd be surprised at how many girls bend the rules.'

My colleagues told me that the clients would try to break me. Told me how they lie. I'm prepared for it. I'm not falling for his game. I lean down, graze my nipples over the shining tip of his straining cock and look up at him.

'Sorry, Steve.'

'Mark,' he pants.

'Sorry, Mark, you'll have to make do with just imagining how good I taste.' I stand up on the table, step up carefully until my feet rest on either side of his head, then I turn around, bending way, way over to grab his cock. He groans as I slip my oil-soaked hands over him. He comes pretty quickly. I like the feeling it gives me, to make a grown man quiver with just the touch of my hand, with just the glimpse of my cunt. The power is like a kind of drug, and we all know how much I like those.

Drugs! I fucking love them.

Here's my brief history of drugs up until this point.

My first cigarette was at twelve. It was a clove cigarette with a sugared tip shared with my best friend Renee. It was amazing. My next cigarette, a stolen Peter Jackson, was not so great, but it didn't matter. I was in! Smoking filled up something inside me, something that had always been missing. It became my lover and my best friend. Until I'm old enough to buy them myself, I go to extreme lengths for cigarettes. Beg, borrow, steal. Get them out of the bin. Pick half-smoked butts out of the gutter. I have no shame, only need.

The first time I smoked pot I was fifteen and with Renee again. I stole it from the woman I babysat for, in tiny, unnoticeable increments. Renee and I smoked it out of the window in my bathroom while my mum was at work, and then, because it was hardcore chronic hydro, we became incredibly paranoid and turned on the hot water, hoping the swirl of steam would blow away the smell, which it did not. My first taste of marijuana felt like coming home. Like something that had always been missing from me was finally there. It became my lover and my best friend. I stole it from everywhere I could because I had no money, no shame, only need.

The first time I took acid was at sixteen, an entire year before I'd even had a drink. It was with my friend Cat on a trip to Sydney, and I wigged out, in a good way. Kind of. I first had ecstasy at the Big Day Out when I was seventeen, split with some stranger in a mosh pit, and the day turned to pure crimson and gold and I felt better than I had ever, ever felt. The first time I took speed I don't actually remember, but I just loved sticking it up my nose so much that every time I did it, I always did too much, and ended up quivering and sick, my nose raw and throat sucked dry. The first time I shot up was behind a church in Surry Hills, at eighteen, with two hardcore junkies I'd met at Centrelink. It wasn't about the drug, it was about the needle. I needed to feel it inside my arm. They missed my notoriously fucking awful veins and it turned my arms black and blue.

Drugs! I love them. They are my lovers and my best friends. I take them at every opportunity.

I have no shame, only need.

* * *

'She's here!'

'Who?' I ask. I'm up on the bench in the kitchen by the window, smoking, and now Sandy is here and she's bouncing with excitement.

'Zara!'

Holy shit! I butt my smoke out badly and move at a hasty pace towards the lounge.

Surrounded by a number of overstuffed bags is a small, olive-skinned woman with wavy, streaked hair. She's wearing a cream-coloured bra, mesh top, very high heels, and an incredibly small G-string, all perfectly coordinated. Her arse is resplendent. Her hair is massive. She exudes kindness and confidence and a sort of jangly energy. She exudes everything. Her limbs are smooth and brown and look like they might feel like butter. I want to touch her, but not like *that*. I do not instantly desire this woman. She is beyond attraction, beyond paltry notions like *fucking*.

I want to *be* this woman.

'Hi,' I say, nervous that she might spot all the ways I am imperfect and do not belong here. I don't know why I am afraid of her, but I am. She's too perfect, too exquisite, too everything. 'I'm Sasha.'

'I'm Zara!'

'I know,' I say and regret it instantly. She gives me a quick, confused look followed by a bright smile, her lovely eyes crinkling, and she sits down at the makeup table, skin glowing in the bulb lights.

Shit. I was about to do that too. *Don't be weird, Sasha.*

Zara pulls out a set of brushes and delves into a makeup bag the size of a small suitcase. I empty out my feeble cosmetics and start to smear foundation onto my acne-scarred cheeks. My lack of expertise fills me with weird shame. Shit, she's looking at me.

'I don't do this makeup thing very often,' I tell her.

'Want some help?' she asks, brightly. She doesn't wait for me to answer, just scoots her chair over and turns me towards her. She assesses my face and gives me another one of those megawatt smiles. Not like I'm pathetic. Not like I don't belong. Like we are friends. Like we are just two gals helping each other out, though I'm not sure what I am helping her with at all. What help could she possibly need from someone like me?

She smooths a finger over my eyebrows.

'Have you ever plucked them?'

I have not. They are huge and a mess. I shake my head, like this is something shameful.

'Want me to?'

*Yes. I want that more than anything in the world.* She approaches me with tweezers and the sharp, eye-water sting comes again and again as she rips the dark hairs from my brow. It hurts but I want to bear it for her. I want to be strong for her. She's got this something that makes me want to do better. Having her so close to my face is horrifyingly thrilling, and it gets all mixed up in the pain from her plucking, so that I am confused and hurt, but excited.

She takes my makeup and I close my eyes and let her brush it softly over my face. She smells amazing too, I knew she would. She smells like expensive perfume, but not overwhelmingly so, just enough. Her gentle hand fills in all the cracks and crevices in my face and, when she's done, she plants a kiss on my forehead.

'Perfect,' she says.

I look. I'm a masterpiece. She's worked miracles. I am a different person. I am a better person. She's masked all the stuff I don't want anyone to see and made me into something aspirational.

'Thank you,' I say. It's not enough.

I make a lot of money on shift, not just because I look gorgeous but because she imbues me with something else. It's like Zara took some of her magic and brushed it onto me with one of her silky makeup brushes.


The owner of the massage parlour, Calvin, is a rotund man with an intense comb-over. He does a lot of speed. I hang out with him at his place sometimes. He teaches me photoshop and HTML, lets me fuck around with the website. Everyone thinks I'm fucking him, but I'm not. I do like his drugs though. That's why I hang out with him.

It's a tale as old as time.

Oh, speed. If I just do a little bit, I become a normal person. The acid-drips down the back of my nose send a sweet calm and sense of well-being to wash over me like a silky wave. But I can't just do a little bit; there's no such thing as a little bit of drugs to me. I sniff and sniff until I feel hideous and sick, but still don't stop. I hide in the bathroom at work and cut copious lines, loving the way I make the powder vanish, loving the way I suck and pull at the inside part where my nose meets my throat till it's raw. The way that too much speed makes me feel terrible and wonderful at the same time is a sick drawcard. Feeling good and shit simultaneously is a common theme with me and drugs. I do this thing where I take way too many drugs, then feel awful and wish I hadn't, hanging on by my fingertips until the effect wears off. Then I do it all again. Why I do this to myself I do not know. I guess I like the pain of it. When I feel mentally terrible, having something that makes me feel physically terrible helps to legitimise it, gives me something to really *feel*.

Calvin cuts up huge creeping columns of amphetamine on CD cases with a slick black credit card. We get all het up and take photos for the website, my naked body shining with grapeseed oil. I wonder what Serena, his co-owner and girlfriend, thinks of this while she's up the road, doing reception at the parlour while he teaches me code and gets me naked for pictures. He does it all the time, with everyone, so it must be fine. *It's fine.* Just do more speed.

Serena is a former worker and a beauty. We all wonder what she's doing with Calvin, but they seem devoted to each other, despite Calvin's penchant for doing lots of drugs with young, scantily clad sex workers. She does speed too, but is much more discreet about it. I see her do it only once, when we share a couple of lines in the office during a shift. She sweeps her long brown hair back and daintily takes a normal, human-sized line up her nose. Serena seems the type to know when enough is enough. She exerts an aura of self-control and calm beauty. I actually really like her, but because I'm such an epic fuck-up, calling in sick all the time, doing drugs all through my shifts, I'm a bit scared of her.

I'm scared of everyone who seems to have their shit together.

So where is my boyfriend in all this?

Well, Leo does what all discriminating adult boyfriends of teenage sex workers do and quits his job to concentrate on his 'music'.

It sounds terrible because it is really, really terrible. Leo finds a way to explain it that makes perfect sense to me. *Of course you need to focus, of course you should just quit and I'll support us. Good idea!* I'm making decent money considering we live like trashbag humans and our most extravagant expense is drugs. There is no way that this can go wrong.

Of course, it does go *very wrong*.

But it takes a while.

There's this feeling in my gut that our relationship is wrong, *very wrong*.

I knew it from the moment I slept with him, the moment I first woke up next to him. He refused to specify himself as my 'boyfriend' for so long that one morning I told him, 'Either we make this a thing, or you can stop sleeping in my goddamned bed every night.'

I make him sound fucking terrible, but I am no angel in all of this either. I am hysterical, often, and not in the way that women are portrayed as 'hysterical' to dismiss their valid concerns (though that is totally a thing I go through too), but actually *hysterical*, screaming and writhing. I sometimes take so many drugs that I become semi-psychotic. One night I come to and find myself carrying a knife up the stairs. Who was it for? Me, or him?

We kinda love each other, in a weird and twisted way. He does little acts of kindness here and there, as I do too. He brings me hot chocolate from the cafe because he knows I hate coffee. He whips up pasta dishes and tries to make me eat them, though I don't often eat. He encourages me to write, brings me drinks and snacks, and lit cigarettes for me to smoke in the bathtub during my epic soaks. Before he quits his job, I fall asleep on the couch on nights when he works so that he can wake me up gently when he gets home, and I can see him before we both go to sleep.

Oh Leo. I know I need him, need someone older to take care of me, teach me how to be a grown-up. It's just that he's not the best teacher and I'm not the best student. We are both doing our best, but we are both terrible in our own ways, and we know it.

It's doomed from the beginning and we know it.

But we keep at it anyway.

I often forget about the work.

Like, not about work itself, but I sort of forget that going to work involves seeing clients in order to make money. When I leave the house, I'm thinking more about hanging out with the other women and seeing my friends, than the whole 'doing sex stuff for money' part of the job.

I'm lonely. I don't have a lot of friends. People can't deal with my unpredictability, oddness and the way that I spend most of my time punching bucket bongs in my living room. It's just not normal. So, the camaraderie that exists between the women at work is, for me, a replacement for having real friends. At work, I'm on my best behaviour. Well, I behave as well as I am able.

But the customers exist there too.

What I can't understand, even while I'm doing the job, is why they don't see a full-service sex worker and get the whole thing. I just can't make sense of how my job even exists.

One guess is that some men don't like the idea of buying actual sex, but they still want to pay a woman to help them ejaculate, so erotic massage is the lesser of two evils. I know that kind of cognitive dissonance.

The average client is in his late thirties to early forties, an office worker from the high-rises close by in North Sydney, or a tradie just finished work. Often, he is called Steve or Mark, John or Mohammad. He wants a pretty girl to rub all up on him for a bit, help him relax. And also orgasm, that is important too.

Other typical customers are older dudes, lonely ones who just want to spend some time with a pretty girl, you know, chat a bit, and maybe get their junk played with. There's randier old guys who are in it for the 'erotic' part of 'erotic massage'. Their hands wander and I have to slap them away. I have a stable of regular older clients who I call 'the creepy uncles', who seem to take great interest in my youngness. There are also a few old fellas who take such sheer delight in the essence of my youth and my touch that I can't help but be affected by their joy.

Rarely, not often, a woman will come in as part of a couple. We workers get in a tizzy when this happens. Well, I know I do. See, most penises are easy to get off. I am an expert hand-job giver at this point. Cisgender women don't just get off with an easy-to-gauge pattern of stroking; they require so much more. You have to watch her body, her breath. Be in tune with her movements, the sounds she makes. Getting her off with your hand is an artform, and I'm much less well practised at it. When a woman comes in, I desperately want to see her, while also desperately hoping she picks someone else.

The first woman I see comes in late one Thursday night, alone and smiling, her grin revealing a missing premolar. She looks like any standard mum from my friends' places years ago. She's fat, middle-aged, blonde and excitable, not like the usual nervous women who come in, most often clutching the arms of a male partner. Some of my fellow workers won't even meet her.

'It's just weird, her coming in alone.'

'Why is it so weird?' I ask.

'Dunno. Just is.'

I mean, compared to our usual clientele, it is a little weird, but there's nothing wrong with it, so I go in and meet her.

'Hi, I'm Sasha.'

'Oh, you look a bit like my daughter!' she says. Damn it, there goes my chance at this booking. Imagine my surprise when Lee comes back in and says that she's chosen me for an hour. I rumple my forehead in confusion, but go and collect her, take her back into one of the massage rooms and instruct her to shower.

'No worries, I know the drill, love,' she says.

Sharon is so different from our usual female clients because of her complete and utter lack of shame. She's joyous, loud and lovely. I start out in the usual way, massaging her back, moving my way slowly to her front, then I douse myself in oil and climb aboard. When our bodies meet, skin to skin, she sighs. She's so silky under my body, soft and slippery, and I wish all my clients felt so good to touch.

I leave a good fifteen minutes for the final section of the session: I have no idea how long she might take to get off. I slide down from her and wash the oil from my hands before I begin to touch her lightly. Between the folds of her cunt she's slick in a different way to the cheap massage oil. She closes her eyes, instantly moans and quivers, then quakes and comes violently. It's unexpected, so fast, like an explosion. Like a plane hitting the side of a mountain and bursting into flames. The burning pieces of her fall back to earth slowly, it takes longer for her to recover than it did to get her there.

'Oh, darl, that was lovely,' she says, jolly to the end.

While there's a large percentage of what you might call 'typical' clients, there are just as many men and women who come to the parlour for 'non-typical' reasons. Couples who aren't quite ready for an all-the-way threesome, or who can't find their 'unicorn'. Younger, stoned guys who want to enhance their mellow. Once, a fellow sex worker came in for a massage and a chat because she was new in town and lonely. Some come for the arse-groping, the tit-grabbing, the dick-pulling; some for the company and a good chat. I like most of them, for different reasons. I do my best to give a good service, it's a service industry after all. I like being sexy, I like being an object for them, or a friendly ear, or a cheeky brat. Whatever they want.

With no sense of self, it's easy for me to fall into the role they want from me.

'You've got to eat something,' Leo says, spreading cream cheese on a blueberry bagel at the cafe.

*Do I, though?*

'Nah,' I say. 'I'm not hungry.' This is a lie. I *am* hungry, I am *always* hungry, but I love the way that not eating makes me feel hollow, light-headed, airy.

I've never not had an eating disorder. When I do eat, I eat like an unsupervised child. Mars Bars for breakfast, hot chips for dinner, endless baguettes. I don't know how to nourish myself. I don't consume a vegetable for years. Food is an afterthought. I go through phases, bingeing and denying. At this stage of my life, I'm on a 'not eating' jag. I maybe eat an apple and a piece of toast in a week. If I think I'm going to faint, I drink a carton of chocolate milk. I whittle down from chunky to svelte, then to far too skinny. My head seems massive atop my spindly body, which matches the way I feel, with all the huge emotions thrashing in my mind. My breasts, once resplendent, wither and fade, hanging like empty sacks.

Sure, it's about control. Sure, it's about a disordered view of my own body. But when I really think about it, not eating is just another way to punish myself. I'm always looking for more of those.

'Just a bite?' Leo asks, holding the glistening bagel in front of me, the sugary, purplish circle heaped with peaks and valleys of brilliant white cream cheese.

'Okay, one bite.' I gingerly nibble a tiny bit off the edge. My mouth instantly floods with saliva, my stomach clamouring for more.

*No. You are a bad person, you do not deserve food.*


Indulge is just down the street, but it could be on another planet, as far as the women who work at Slide are concerned.

'*Blow jobs!*' they hiss. '*Extras.*'

But when it slows for me at Slide after a few months, a new girl called Charlotte – a beautiful bulimic who I've glommed to since her first night – suggests we go down the road to Indulge and see if they're hiring.

Ha, *if*. Massage parlours are *always* hiring.

'You don't have to do extras, apparently,' Charlotte says. 'But think of the money.'

I do think of the money, and I remember how taking a dick in my hand and pulling on it for money felt pretty normal the first time I did it. Who knows? Maybe other things will be the same. Who am I to judge? Full service – I don't think that's for me, but I feel like everything else is fair game. It's as if I'm tip-toeing around the boundaries of what I can handle, what I'll give, and I like that. I like dancing on the edge of things.

Even though I have a giant cold sore when I show up for the interview, they don't seem to mind. They hire us on the spot, roster us a few shifts.

'Don't touch it,' says the woman who meets us, referring to the pulsing scab on my face.

'Yes, I know, I won't.'

It clears before my first shift, and I dab makeup on the tiny red scar it leaves in a new staff lounge, under different lights. There are so many women here, it lacks the family atmosphere of Slide but feels more like a real business. There's no one offering amphetamines from the door of the office, no workers snarfing up lines in the bathroom that I know of, except for me.

Indulge has lots more rooms, tiny little closets for sharing secrets. Just enough room to do the job, no more. A massage table, towels, a clock and passage to move around the client. It's best if he just lies down real quick.

And it is *busy*.

Charlotte and I are slammed from the moment we walk in the door. Fresh flesh always starts out busy, and I'm not minding. Well, I'm kind of minding. I'd love a minute to sit down, have a smoke and a chat with the women who populate this particular parlour, but I'm too busy racing between bookings, mopping up the makeup sliding down my face from the human-to-human humidity, and slipping in and out of heels and lingerie.

All this work is really fucking with my ability to enjoy work.

Slide is *never* this busy. With this smorgasbord of women available just up the road, why would it be? Indulge is older, more established, and while the rooms are smaller, they are nicer, more uniform, like a well-oiled hand-job factory. Every kind of woman in all colour combinations stalks the halls. And they do things, *other things*, quite openly and without shame.

And so do I.

Mostly, the men at Indulge just want to go down on me, which is A-okay. Please do! And I get fifty bucks? Fucking awesome. One guy wants me to perform oral on him, so I slip a condom over his cock, open my mouth and look up into his eyes. He lasts all of ten seconds. It feels like a line that I cross over in a quick-step motion and it's easy. It's nothing. Nothing except money and I like money. I like counting it afterwards. It feels like the kind of money I *deserve*. I work hard for this and it's beautiful and precious.

I come home reeking of massage oil, shuffling fifty-dollar notes.

All this cash doesn't make me quit Slide. I split the week: sitting round, snarfing lines and chatting with the women at Slide, quietly adoring Zara from afar, then I hustle down to Indulge once or twice a week for big cash, where I have to snort lines in the bathroom like some kind of secret drug addict.

Then Zara quits.

*Where did she go?* It's like a contained explosion and the hallways of Slide are filled with delicious hearsay and conjecture. I am bereft. I miss her perfectly coordinated outfits, big hair and kindness. Slide feels hollow without her, and suddenly takes on this seedy vibe – the mural on the wall in room two is tacky as shit, that little room at the back that the creepiest clients like because of the closeness of the mirrors is no longer quirky but claustrophobic.

Out of nowhere, Zara calls me on my stocky little blue Nokia.

'The place I'm working at is so much fucking nicer than Slide. You should come and try it.'

Zara is a savvy business woman above anything else. A workaholic and a dedicated employee, she has some regular office-type job that she goes to in the day, and works a few nights making fast cash with her hands. And she makes a fuckton of cash. She's the perfect ten of massage parlour work.

Every parlour has its top earner. She's their biggest money-maker on whatever shift she works. She's in possession of particular attributes that make her the perfect sex worker. They are as follows:

1. Really good looking. Doesn't have to be blonde or even too slim, not at all; just really beautiful in her own unique way. Inner beauty counts too.
2. A workaholic.
3. Good to clients. Not in any 'special favours' way, but *good* to them. She cares deeply for them, or pretends to care to such a degree that it's impossible to tell she's faking.
4. Has a great well inside her that she can pull from to feed men's neediness.

The last one is so important. Most sex workers need this well in them, and if they don't have it, they won't last long. Men's neediness can suck a worker dry. It's not just their need – that's just the word I use for it – it's their desire, their particular thing that sucks at a worker and requires fulfilment. I'm not saying that men are psychic vampires, not at all. Everyone sucks and gives in their own way: man, woman or other. But when you're being paid for sex or sex-like activities, you feel each client's void. You fill it, anywhere up to eight voids a night. It can be draining.

Zara was Slide's top earner, so when she left it rocked the house into chaos. I'm keen to be out of there, anyway. The drugs are out of control, everyone thinks I'm fucking Calvin, and it's so quiet that I have to bolster my income with men's heads between my legs at Indulge more and more often.

A new job is as good as a new ... everything. I can fashion whatever persona I like, slip out of 'mad, drug-addicted teenager who is supposedly fucking the boss' (I swear, I never did!) and shake myself into a new shape. When Zara calls and tells me to come over to Boutique, that it's better and busier there, I say, 'Why not?' and arrange an interview.

'Arranging an interview' is basically being hired. I know now that any massage parlour I walk into will hire me on the spot, because I'm reasonably pretty and want to do the work. They are the only prerequisites.

I catch the bus out to a suburb I've never heard of and suddenly I'm an employee of Boutique. It's that simple.

Boutique is beautiful compared to the dingy interiors of Slide and the factory-farm-like atmosphere of Indulge. It is a 'no-extras' parlour and busy enough to make up for that, financially. It sits above a post office and next to a children's dance school. Boutique and the school share a stairwell that is dutifully blocked off with shadecloth to protect the customers and the children from crossing paths. The interior is all fake marble, with spacious rooms lined in mirrors (always, the mirrors) and set out with giant spas.

Fuck, I love a good spa. You can run one of those bitches and then spend the hour splashing around with the client, doing not much else, making dollars to essentially take a bath with a strange man. 'How about we have a spa?' becomes one of my most common questions, and the answer is often yes.

It's like the beautiful surrounds and fresh start make me want to try to be a better person. My drug use stays off premises, unlike the other parlours where I've spent nights sniffing rails off my makeup mirror in the toilets. After all, Zara vouches for me here, and I want to make a good impression for her.

Zara quickly becomes Boutique's top earner. She even has clients who follow her over from the North Shore, she's that good. It would be easy to hate her for this, to be jealous, but she's just too lovely. In her perfect outfits, with her mass of hair, she radiates warmth from her fine-limbed frame. She dazzles the soft light of the girls' lounge whenever she's in it. I'm perfectly happy to be in orbit around her. And, taking in my fresh, new, faux-marble surrounds, I'm glad I've followed her.

And then, Leo fucks my best friend.

The one I mentioned before – my first cigarette, first joint. We've known each other since we were quite young.

I tell him, 'Please, just not her,' after the first time, but he does it again, despite my protests. I am furious.

'Please, just not her,' I tell him.

I'm all for open relationships, but she's my *best friend*, since we were *little kids*, and I'm wondering why he can't just find some other chick, one who means less to me, to stick his overworked penis into. Also, they get along really well. Their interests align outside the sexual realm, which is something I can't say for Leo and me. I never thought I'd say it in reference to myself, but I am deeply, deeply jealous. Not just of him being with her, but of her being with him. And not me. *I* need to be the centre of this world, and I'm not. They are developing something special, something that I'm not a part of and it hurts so badly.

'Please, just not her,' I plead.

I embark on a series of intense outbursts in order to protest this situation. I fuck whomever, hoping to make them jealous. I cut myself to ribbons and overdose on Xanax so they can find me, limp and bleeding, in the shower. I lose my shit one day and stab the floor of my bedroom over and over with a kitchen knife, making invisible cuts in the carpet that no one can see, but that I know are there.

Please, just not her. Fuck anyone: my ex-lover from high school (he does), the scores of worker-babes I bring home for drug-fuelled orgies (he does), random strangers we pick up wherever (he does.) But he fucks her too, and it twists me deep inside. It gnaws. I am a supernova of jealousy. Something dies in my friendship with Renee, something that won't rekindle for a decade or more, and I blame Leo for the loss of a kinship that was so integral to my life, so special.

Please, just not her.

The only place to smoke at Boutique is in the stairwell right by the front door. This is the same stairwell that sits right next to the stairwell to the dance school. The shadecloth protects us from sight, but I can't imagine our raucous conversations about drugs and dicks are as well concealed. I smoke outside with Ellie, an ectomorphic mother-of-one, and Rose, a ruddy brunette from the western suburbs. I'm still sporting my goth look, Snow White with a ciggie hanging from her lips, but Boutique is an 'evening dress' parlour. Parlours are always one or the other – 'dress' or 'lingerie' – and there are hard and fast rules about adhering to the dress codes. So, no flouncing about, meeting clients in lingerie here; our lingerie is underneath a variety of short tight cocktail-style dresses. Mine is a strange green-and-cream print, which is hideous, but the cut hugs the planes of my body well and makes my tits look amazing without a bra, so it doesn't hinder my earning potential. I've got these pointy black leather heels with a cuff around the ankle, which I got off a 'shopper' who came by the parlour in my early days at Boutique.

'Shoppers' are actually shoplifters. They thieve and then bring around huge bags of their wares to parlours and sell the booty to women who can overlook the dubious origins for big, big savings! Perfume, makeup, lingerie, shoes, dresses. For some reason no shoppers ever stopped by Slide or Indulge (or maybe they just didn't let them in), so it's an entirely new phenomenon for me, and I fucking love it. Suddenly I have a bunch of nice makeup, designer perfumes, cute dresses – and there's just something about lovely stuff that makes me feel good. Adds to the mask, makes it fit better. There are nights when I spend most of my earnings on shopper stuff, because who knows when they might be back? These babes could be busted at any time. It's quite a sight to see a gaggle of sex workers falling onto a freshly poured-out mound of stolen cosmetics like starving dogs onto a fresh kill.

I do a lot of day shifts at Boutique, even though Zara works most often at night. I like the place in the daytime. All the other parlours are devoid of natural light, except for the kitchen at Slide, so the sunlight coming through the windows in Boutique's staff lounge, and the warm sun coming through the shadecloth as we smoke on the steps, makes the whole place feel brighter and more friendly.

I like Boutique. The pay is good and the women are lovely and engaging. It feels neither scummy nor like a hand-job factory. On one of my first days, Grace and Lily are narrating the runways on Fashion TV in indeterminable international accents.

'You are too wide, Naomi,' they say as we giggle in the background. 'You will burst my expensive Italian clothes.'

Grace is a bombshell-bodied Eurasian – DDs in perfect proportion with the rest of her. I am besotted at once, and almost die when I get to do a double with her. She writhes exquisitely as she rubs the poor guy down. I barely notice him but take in every inch of her and commit it to my long-term memory, knowing it is too good to let the drugs scramble. The exact pitch of her skin, the natural, subtle curl of her hair, the way her lips O when she lets out another of those fake moans. I never let her know how fascinated I am by her. Grace is not quite in the realm of Zara, who is too perfect to touch. I very much want to fuck Grace, but I'm terrified that she's too together and responsible to mess around with the likes of me. I don't even know if she's bisexual, but the odds are good that she's open – so many workers I meet are, if not straight-out bisexual, queer, gay or lesbian, at least bi-curious. Even with those odds, I still don't tell her. I'm so shit at letting people know I like them. Usually I just get fucked up and take my clothes off in an inappropriate place. If they react favourably, then that's a good indication that they're into me. You wouldn't think this method a practical one, but it's worked well for me up until this point, so why change it?

Grace takes me by the chin one day and tells me, 'You're beautiful. I mean it. You are, like, movie pretty.' I don't know how she can tell that I think I'm hideous, but it's as though she reads me plain as words in the sky. She knows what I need to hear. It thrills me, terrifies me. She sees me.


Occasionally at Boutique large groups of men will come in together. Two or three is strange but not uncommon, but five or more is irregular and strikes me as weird. Like, how do you bring that up with a group of friends? 'Wanna go for a quick dick-pulling at the local rub and tug?'

There's nothing that requires fortitude as much as entering a room where five guys are waiting to assess you. Being stared at by one client is hard enough, but five pairs of eyes on me is a lot of eyes. Plus, it's scary. It's me against these men, this *pack*, and as I clack into the room in my heels I feel the power imbalance like a physical entity.

'What's your name?' one of them asks me.

'What do you do?' another says before I have a chance to answer.

I bite my tongue, because I know what I want to say, but I need the money and can't afford to insult these men. Plus, if I bite, they might bite back. There sure are a lot of them, and only one of me.

There's a guy sitting off to the side, who says nothing. He's got a stack of fifties in his hand, and he's tapping it against his palm. It's several thousand bucks, easily. He must be footing the bill, then. He looks me up and down, still tapping the wad of money. It glows yellow, a fistful of pineapples. What is this? Why does he need to flash this wad of cash at me?

'I'm Sasha,' I say. 'I'm a lot of fun.' There's an edge to my voice that I'm hoping says, 'Do not fuck with me,' but is more likely just a nervous pitch.

'I bet you are,' the ringleader says. Tap, tap, tap.

I don't have anything more to say. I want to be out of the room, right now, so I turn on my heel and walk out, feeling their eyes on my back.

Later, when the deal has been done, the receptionist comes in and reels off a list of names. I'm one of them, to my surprise.

'The big man,' the receptionist says. 'He wants to see you.'

Me?

I walk in as the other women take their clients out and there he is, waiting for me. The ringleader. That stack of fifties in his hand is smaller, but there's still some there. Who is this guy?

'So, you're a lot of fun, hey?'

'Yeah,' I challenge him.

He tucks the fifties away and I lead him to the room. I show him just how fun I can be, and he leaves a couple of the crisp fifties on the massage table for me in return.


Leo and I break up in relatively unspectacular fashion. I am sick of his everything, as he is of mine, though the first thing he says after we break up is, 'Do you want to have sex?', to which I respond only by screaming hysterically. Neither of us has the money to move, and the house is technically his place, in as much as a rental can be anyone's. So we still share a room, and the way we hate each other pulses in the space between us on the bed, which we widen every day.

Zara can see the cracks are starting to show. 'Come stay at my place for the week,' she says. 'We can work the whole time, make a bunch of cash and you can move out.'

I am speechless with gratitude. Why is she doing this? Most people I know cannot stand the chaotic mess I have become, or they have drifted away, scared of watching me fling myself headlong into destruction. It's like Zara sees me or sees through the threads of havoc I've thrown up all around myself. She sees through the mess and thinks there might be something more.

Even though I usually only do what is worst for myself, and rarely accept help, I take up her offer and spend a blissful week away from Leo.

Zara lives in a lovely little flat close to her parents' place, and she and her mother take care of me, the way I'd wanted Leo, or indeed anyone, to take care of me. Zara has quit her day job by this point and so we plan a full week of work. Her professionalism must rub off on me or something because the clients respond with fistfuls of dollars. I make enough to move out, and more.

In the evenings at her home, she and her mother feed me delicious roasted chicken and potatoes. She tells me her story and her history. I don't tell anyone what she shares with me, and I won't say it here. Zara goes from my idol to someone real and layered. She's off the pedestal and on a more equal footing to myself – though still above me. Perhaps I'm just kneeling at her feet now.

This week shows me something: that I am indeed worthy of love and care. I feel the care that Zara has for me deeply, and I fight it for the first few days. It hurts and feels wrong for anyone to love me. When she hugs me I go rigid. In the sweet-smelling, tidy space of Zara's flat I do battle with myself and my utter loathing. The love I let in in tiny bites eats at the way I hate myself. It is terrifying. It is scary to feel good about myself. Even the snippets of her mother caring for me have a deep and profound impact. I am not used to being taken care of. I crave it and search for it, but really, I'm looking to be mistreated, 'cause I'm twisted like that. I think it's all I deserve. To feel real care and to allow it in? This is revelatory.

I don't know why I fucking hate myself.

But I do. If you asked me for a list of what I liked about myself, I could rattle off a few things. I have great tits. I'm okay at the whole writing thing. I'm really good at Scrabble. But if you asked me what I don't like about myself, I could go on forever.

Here's what I know: when I look in the mirror, I want to break it. Half the time when I open my mouth, I think, *Shut up, you stupid fucking bitch, no one wants to hear you speak.* I hate myself so thoroughly that I seek out my own personal degradation – I'll not only let anyone do anything to me, I'll participate enthusiastically in it, because I can't imagine how anyone would want to be around me otherwise. I score my own body with lighters and razors for a lot of reasons, but also because I feel like I deserve nothing but pain and scars. The hate I feel for myself stings and sears. It razes through me like fire across a field left to crackle in the sun. I am useless, worthless, nothing but a pain to be around. I don't just hate myself, I *loathe* myself. I deserve everything terrible that happens to me, and more.

The week at Zara's goes far too quickly and going back to Leo's feels like a step backwards, as though I'm jumping into a fast-running river of misery. I look at apartments, but everything I can afford is hideous and I just can't decide between the revolting hovels presented to me. One is a single room the size of a shoebox with a tiny sink, a microwave in the corner, and a filthy bathroom down the hall; another is bigger and self-contained, but with a huge pile of garbage in the centre of the room. The weeks tick by and Leo and I dance around each other, falling into bed now and then, which spurs a ridiculous new level of hatred of myself. The rest of the time we do not speak to each other. The care I felt with Zara and her family, the rosy glow it left, dims and dims.

One night I sit up in the bedroom, crying softly to myself,

Leo having claimed the lounge room before I came home from work. I desperately call everyone in my phone and, when no one answers, I take every single pill in arm's reach, about fifty or so of varying kinds. Just as I swallow the last one down, Charlotte calls. Even though we banded together for our first shifts at Indulge, she's really only an acquaintance and it's weird and wrong that I have reached out to her like this, left that tearful message on her phone. I tell her what I have done, and she begins to freak out.

'I'm calling you an ambulance,' she says as I beg her not to. 'This is completely manipulative,' she says before she hangs up. 'Never call me again.'

There's not much else for it, so I slit my wrists and surprise my housemates when paramedics knock on the door and ask about the girl who is overdosing upstairs. Look, it is a quiet overdose.

When you overdose on purpose, people at the hospital will be mean to you. The nurse who is ordered to bandage my wrists sighs and does it without looking at me.

Because I'm still conscious, they hand me cup after cup of liquid charcoal, which I vomit in great inky draughts all over myself. Every time I spew one up, they hand me another until I keep them down.

'I need to talk to someone,' I tell another nurse, but no one comes to talk to me. I lie in bed all night, the beep of my heart monitor making it hard to sleep. What also makes it hard to sleep are the thoughts and feelings that won't stop blooming inside me as I gradually sober up. I'm miserable, bereft. And fucking lonely. All that help Zara granted me, all her love and effort, it feels completely wasted by this act. What was I doing? How did I think that this would help?

As the clock ticks painfully slow, I begin to make decisions. I have to. No one else is going to fix this.

*Okay, Mia. You can't stay at Leo's any more. You need to get out. Today. Right now. You can't keep doing the same thing if you want your life to be different.*

As the sun rises, I rip out all my wires and leave without telling the nurses. I buy a pack of cigarettes at the closest convenience store, sit at a bench by a real-estate agent's office and smoke until they open. They're the ones who showed me the garbage pile house. I tell the freshly put-together agent that I want to take the apartment as I pick at the sticky ECG stickers on my chest.

'Can I move in today?' I ask her.

'Um, okay,' she says.

I pay my money, she gives me a set of keys.

On my way home, I pull a tag off a flyer on a pole and call the number. The 'man with the van' says he can come by later that day. I tiptoe into the house and pack up everything I own. It's pretty meagre. Thankfully, Leo has a job again and is at work, so I don't need to explain myself to him, because fuck, what would I say? Sorry? Better to just disappear.

The van man arrives, and I help him load the stuff into his beat-up Mitsubishi Express. He politely attempts to not look at the bandages on my wrists and doesn't say anything about the pile of trash in the new apartment, for which I am eternally grateful.

When he leaves, I package up the garbage and put it into the bins out the front. I unpack my things and sit in the apartment, smoking furiously. I look around: there's a bookcase with a few books on it, a futon mattress on the floor, a plastic box with a shitty little TV on top. That's it. This is my new life. I start to cry. I keep crying for a few weeks in between punching endless bongs and my shifts pulling dick at the parlour. I'm on my own for the first time ever. I have no one to take care of me.

Looks like that's up to me now.

I have just turned twenty years old.

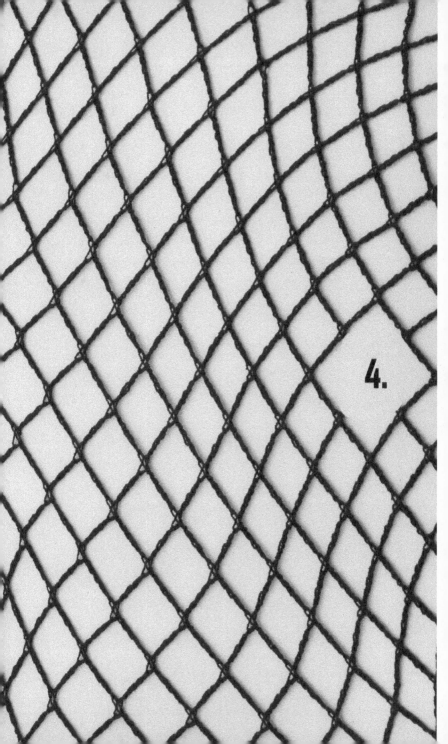

4.

At Boutique someone brings in a bag of work-suitable clothes (a 'whoredrobe') they don't want any more, and every woman in the house digs through like their very lives depend on it. The small bright staff lounge fills up with errant slips of fabric, the moulded cups of push-up bras. I stand to the side, letting the alphas have first feed, picking up the cast-offs. Someone chucks a pink beaded number my way and, though pink isn't really my thing, I hold it up to the light. It's pale pink, Caucasian skin-coloured almost. The fabric is a wide mesh and I go through my stuff until I find a nude G-string. I put it on and assess myself in the mirror.

'Keep that,' Grace says. 'You look amazing.'

'I look naked,' I say. 'Naked and sparkly.'

But my ensemble has the approval of Grace and thus, it is done. I step into my heels and prance about the lounge, to approving calls and wolf-whistles. Not long after, the doorbell rings. After a few minutes the receptionist comes in, telling us there's a customer to meet.

'Sasha first!' Grace says, and I scoot into the waiting room to scattershot giggles. He is seated on the other side of the long room (brothel proportions are always so strange) and when I walk in the door he takes a look at me, pauses a second, and then almost jumps out of his chair.

Later on, after he has chosen me and the deal is done, he says, 'When you walked in the room, I thought you were completely naked. I thought I was going to have a heart attack.'

This is the power of a good dress.

Everyone has their 'money dress'. If you're working in a lingerie parlour, you have your money lingerie set. My first money dress was a sheer mesh nightie that I wore at lingerie parlour Slide. When it died from exposure to massage oil and rough hands, I bought something similar. Because it worked. Money dresses can come from high-end stores, or the bargain bin at a second-hand shop. It doesn't matter where it comes from or how much it costs, only how it makes you feel. If you feel good and hot and sexy, then clients will look at you like you're good and hot and sexy and be more likely to choose you to play with their penis for money.

Skimpy black nighties that allow my lingerie to peek through were fine for lingerie parlours like Slide and Indulge, but at Boutique I gather around me a collection of skin-tight cocktail dresses, wrap dresses that show off my cleavage, and dresses with slits that I complement with stockings and suspenders. There's my green number which is an okay dress because of the cut, a black cocktail dress that seems to inflate my breasts to massive proportions and quickly becomes my new 'money dress', and the mesh number that I end up never wearing aside from that one meeting. That kind of dress might have been okay at a lingerie parlour like Indulge, but not here at Boutique; it makes me look naked and I don't want to be accused of 'sharking'.

Sharking is frowned upon. A classic sharking move would be to defy the rules of the parlour's dress code and try to get away with showing more than the other girls to drum up business and influence the clients for bookings. Also considered sharking: coming out into the hallway in various states of undress to be 'accidentally' exposed to someone's client as they bring them through; offering extras at a no-extras parlour, or offering extras at a reduced rate when they are permissible. It's all considered unfair and anyone accused of sharking will be gossiped about and excluded from the pack.

There are hustlers too. Hustling feels a little like sharking but is actually a completely different thing. A hustler is there to make money, pure and simple, and will do everything it takes to make fistfuls of it. They do intros when they're not available, 'Just to say hello for next time,' and talk the talk when it comes to convincing clients to see them.

There are hustlers who don't shark, and sharkers who aren't hustlers.

I do not shark. I am not good at the hustle, and adopt the 'if they want me, they will pick me; if not, good riddance' approach. It's why I never stripped – I couldn't imagine having to convince people to do anything, let alone pay for my fucking lap dances. After all, *I* simply refuse to do anything I don't want to do, so I get it.

Dresses are fraught for me. They are a play to femininity and used to stand for something that I felt I was separate from, because I was not a 'proper girl'. Lingerie too. Anything that might signify me as someone who cared about how I looked felt insincere to me, because if you don't care about how you look then no one can use the failure of an outfit against you. But here, in these oil-scented halls, dresses take on a new meaning for me. They are a way to enhance my sexuality, to signal to a customer what they could be in for should they choose me. Years later, I will sometimes come across an old work dress and I'll clutch it to me, breathing in the smell of sweat and the particular scent of old massage oil that permeates the fabric. That's the thing: once a work dress, always a work dress. You can't get that smell out. You can't take those feelings out.

\* \* \*

I settle into my new, independent life slowly, like a new couch adapting to a parade of arses. Speaking of couches, or furniture at all, I start a small collection of actual homewares that I collect from kerbside clean-ups. People throw out their trash and I carry it gratefully up to my apartment. An armchair. A full-length mirror. A TV stand. A bookshelf for all my knick-knacks. A real bedframe. My house starts to become a home.

I learn to love living alone. Living alone is perfect if you are incredibly selfish, and I am.

Living alone does not love me. All my worst habits come to the fore because there is no one to silently judge me, no one to try to seem normal for. If I want to punch five bongs before I climb out of bed, so be it. If I want to snort lines of Special K off CD cases on my computer table as I surf the internet, why not? Spend hours in the shower because it calms me: sure! Go for it!

My drug dealer, Dan, lives just around the corner, and we become close, because I always need drugs and he has them. He is also a really nice guy, an older doof-loving hippie and all-around good dude, aside from the drug dealing. We get so familiar with each other that he offers for me to clean his house once a week in return for one hundred dollars' worth of cannabis. What a deal! In addition to that, he's always asking me to help him sample new drugs as he gets them in, and I am a willing test subject. I spend most of my cleaning time zooming about with the vacuum cleaner, scrubbing walls and chewing on the insides of my face.

He is a good man. Maybe he wants to fuck me, maybe not. He never gives me any indication either way and I don't find him predatory at all. I reckon he just thinks I'm a lonely, fucked-up girl in need of some kindness – and he'd be right. He's twice my age and seems to know that, after Leo, I cannot deal with an older man in any sexual shape or capacity … outside of work. That's a different thing.

Dan gets great drugs. Hydro pot *and* bush; a cornucopia of amazing ecstasy pills; sheets of colourful blotter acid; even fucking *microdots*, small black grains like poppyseeds that are potent doses of LSD and incredibly rare. His ketamine is utterly pure, so when my friends try it, they become completely enamoured.

'This is amazing. Can you get some of this for me?'

Why not? Share the love, and the good drug connections! Soon I'm getting on for a couple of different people every week. Dan starts giving me bags at a discount and tells me to pass it on at regular prices and keep the extra money for myself. Don't mind if I do!

And then, suddenly one day, I think, *Am I a drug dealer?*

Do I have customers? Yes.

Do I make money from drugs? Yes.

*Shit.*

I am not responsible enough to be a fucking *dealer*. I am a drug addict! They make the worst dealers! I tell Dave I'm not comfy with this situation and get his permission to give his contact details to my customers. Thus ends my completely accidental foray into dealing drugs. I settle back into my computer chair and snarf up some lines of K, safe in the knowledge that the only drugs in the house are for me. All for me.

Now and then I try a new parlour, just to see what the conditions, the women and the pay are like. There's a place in the CBD (Central Business District) that I've seen as I've passed it on the bus, and I decide to give it a go. It can't hurt to diversify, right?

This place is a dress parlour, but it's unlike any other place I've worked before. The workers all sit in a large open area around a bar, perching awkwardly on stools in their evening dresses and heels, or on couches scattered around, trying to look as if they just happen to be lounging in this forced space. The clients come in and hang out until they meet a girl who they'd like to see, exchange cash and head upstairs to a room for the business to take place. I settle in for my first shift by the bar and spend twenty minutes talking to some guy before another worker dives in and swoops him out from underneath me. He heads upstairs with her, a sick, twisted joy on his face that there have been two women fighting for his measly handful of bucks. What the fuck? And I'm in for eleven more hours of this? I realise that it's every woman for herself, that this is the ultimate shark-tank and I'm gonna have to hustle if I want to make any money at all. But I'm no good at the hustle, right? We've talked about this.

Finally, my charm pays off and a guy decides to see me. I ask him if he has any preference for rooms, but he tells me he wants to get in the hot tub. They'd mentioned this mythical tub on orientation, so I head to the area the receptionist had pointed at and find a huge spa populated with women and their clients. All together. Their bodies up close in the water. Together. There are three women and three clients, all completely naked. My heart sinks and my body floods with dread. The whole spa reeks of chemicals and I hope they're strong enough to kill the millions of bacteria and assorted body-grossness that would populate this warm, wet environment. I dip a toe in and it's like I can feel the germs crawling up my leg.

No. Oh no.

I get in gingerly, my client rubbing my arse under the bubbles. I'm just not prepared for this. He plants my hand on his dick, and I'm thinking, *Oh god, I'm not jerking you off in here, you gross fuck.* I wonder how many of these men expect this, are happy to be sitting in what very well could be jizz-soup, kept piping hot. I smile a strained and hideous smile, and laugh with all the other women and men in the tub but, on the inside, I am dying, dying. When time's up I clamber out as fast as I can and the client suggests another half-hour, seeing as he didn't get his rocks off. I mumble something about a booking and then run as fast as I can to the dressing room, where I dress in under thirty seconds, grab my stuff and head to the front desk.

'I've got an emergency, I need to go.'

The emergency is that I am repulsed and covered in germs.

The receptionist looks at me as though she's extremely disappointed in my work ethic, but she pays me out and I hurry through the door. I catch a passing taxi home, where I spend the next hour in the shower, scrubbing at my body, turning it pink then red, rinsing off the soap and then adding another layer until my bottle of bodywash is half empty.

The next day they call me and tell me they need me again for a night shift.

I politely decline.


I have these episodes I come to call my 'morning fits'. I have no idea what they are. They happen most mornings, beginning not long after I wake up. They start with a gut-jumping sense of doom, like everything is threatening me. The shower. The unmade bed. The cup for my tea. Getting dressed intensifies it, the clothes feeling wrong against my skin. Itchy. Tight. Not tight enough. Not right. The blame then switches to my body. Nothing fits it. My hair will not cooperate. My face is all wrong. I claw at myself, wishing I could be anybody, anyone else. I feel stuck in my body, like, if I could, I'd tear free of it. The feeling trebles, turns red. Turns to a rage so vast that I don't know how the apartment, the block, the whole street isn't shaking. I fume. I rage. I scream silent and long, throw things, and rip other things to shreds. I pull my hair and scratch my nails down my thighs. I stab myself with pens or sewing needles. I ache, I ache, I ache.

And then I start my day.

I know this is not normal, but I don't know that these rage-jags I go on are atypical panic attacks. I don't figure it out for a long time. I just imagine it's more evidence of the fact that I am built wrong.

Damaged.

I've heard it said that every sex worker is damaged in some way, and I'd say that is true – because every single *person* is damaged in some way. Everyone has their baggage, and sex workers are no different.

I can't tell you how many clients have asked me if I was sexually abused. It's an incredibly personal question, but one that is so common I become fucking sick of people asking me that. I mean, fuck, what a thing to ask! We're trying to have a fun, sexy time here! For the record: some of the sex workers I know were. Some weren't. Much like the general population. It's one of the many common misconceptions about sex workers that I come across. Here are some more:

*Sex workers are drug addicts.*

In fact, while some are recreational drug users and some are addicts, a lot of the workers I come across aren't addicts or even recreational users. I, for instance, *am* a drug addict. Many of my co-workers are not. I've done sex work while addicted to drugs and while sober. Again, it's a reflection of the general population. Some people are, some aren't.

*Sex workers are mentally ill.*

Yes, I am mentally ill. Sex work provides, for a time, a refuge job that I can take because I am too mentally ill to hold down a regular job. But not all sex workers are mentally ill. Some are, and some also have chronic illnesses, so they use the job because it's flexible and profitable and a way to make a living that works with their disabilities. The sex workers I meet are about as varied as any group of people in regard to mental illness.

*Sex workers make a tonne of money.*

Not always true. A sex worker's income depends on a varying set of factors that include the personal, the seasonal, the proximity to tax time and holidays, even the fucking weather. There's a rough pattern of ebbs and flows that can be followed, but often it is completely unpredictable. For instance, some summertime Friday nights you'd think would be pumping, I walk away with nothing, having sat on my numb arse for hours with my whoreface on, waiting for work. Some deep winter Monday nights I go home counting my fifties, inhaling the smell of fresh money and getting weirdly turned on by it. You can never tell. It is as complex and unpredictable as men's desires. Most of the time I'm happy as long as I can pay the bills and buy enough drugs and shoes to keep myself amused while not having to work very often. Sometimes there's something I specifically want and I'll set myself a target. I meet women who get into the industry to pay back debts, to save for holidays, to buy a car, a house. I meet women who live frugal and save hard, women who spend all their money on designer clothes and bags, women who pay private school bills with sex work money, and women who shoot every cent they earn into their arms.

There are a few generalisations I would make about sex workers: they are all extremely interesting and complex people. Most of them are good people in their own various ways. They're strong and capable: working a job with not only a high emotional output/input, but a job that receives a great deal of stigma from all sides: the wider world, as well as those close to them. Sometimes even from the receptionists paying them out at the end of the night – even though sex work pays their wages too. Sometimes the stigma comes even from the very people who are consuming their services.

I can't count the number of men who tell me, 'You're too good to do this,' or 'You're too smart to be here,' as if my inherit goodness or intelligence should disqualify me from sex work.

*Fuck off.*

It's as if they think only a certain type of woman should do this kind of work: *bad women*. Yet they're happy to participate, so what does that say about them?

At Christmastime, the owner from Boutique plans a party. Colin is the kind of guy who really likes that he has a stable of beautiful women. He's not a bad guy, just slightly creepy in the way that many men who run sex-work establishments are.

We make him a great deal of money, so he books a table at a fancy restaurant in Balmain for the party and closes Boutique for a rare night. We all rock up in our best dresses, and he dons a tux and sits at the head of the table. The other patrons of the restaurant must wonder who this single man is, in the company of so many beautiful women, all so disparate and dressed to their respective nines. In our group there are sweet long-haired hippies; cropped-haired butch lesbians; women in full goth regalia; ladies in heavy makeup and skin-tight cocktail dresses. We all teeter in heels, cackling, drinking fancy cocktails and nicking outside often for cigarettes and bitch sessions. The restaurant is as cavernous as an aeroplane hangar, modelled with streamlined steel surfaces. The napkins are cloth. A crisp-looking waiter asks me about my wine preferences. I have no idea what to say, so I stare at him until he goes away.

We must look quite the team. Allie tells a rollicking story about giving a guy a vigorous hand-job, making the motions, and several patrons on other tables look scandalised, turning up their noses at this mysterious group of women cutting loose. It's not often we meet up together outside of work and getting the lot of us all in the same place at the same time is a logistical task of magnificent proportions. Usually we are five to a shift, so it's good fun to spend time together that isn't interrupted by clients ringing the doorbell.

I sit close to Zara and Grace and delicately spoon salmon into my red-lipsticked mouth. We sink strawberry daquiris by the half-dozen.

The night is so special to me: it makes me feel like a normal person, the kind of gal who has friends and goes to a work Christmas party. I sip my daquiri, looking up and down the table at all these exquisite women, every one a complex trove of personality and just so cool. And for once I'm fulfilled, so fucking happy to be here, with friends. Or as close to friends as I can get.

Later on, I find out that the drinks bill alone comes to five grand. That's what happens when you take twenty massage-parlour employees out on the town.


Dan drops by with a gram of ketamine for me, and I hand him a bunch of fifties.

'Talk soon,' he says as he leaves, and I know we will. I talk to Dan more than I talk to most of my friends. He probably *is* my closest friend. Or maybe what he gives me – the pills, powders and plants in translucent little bags – are my closest friends. Drugs provide the kind of friendship I'm seeking – intense and constant. No human could be there for me as much as I need them to be; my expectations are utterly unrealistic. I require round-the-clock support. But drugs? As long as I've got enough money, they'll always be there for me.

This ketamine is pure and comes in chunks of crystal. I crush it down to white powder onto a CD case with my bank card, carving tiny lines. I've got the night off work and no idea what to do with myself. My phone's not ringing, no one has responded to my 'I'm bored, wanna hang/fuck?' texts, so it's time to lose a couple of hours.

That's what drugs are to me: a way to pass the time. The time, which clicks by so painfully, every hour a slow drip that eats away at me. Every hour where my phone doesn't chime, every minute that I'm not sure what to do, every second where I have to be alone with myself.

Ketamine produces a gentle rush of not-quite-there that I love. What better way to lose time than powerfully assisted dissociation? And why dissociate for free when I can get such a better quality of being out of my body and brain for a few spare fifties? If I snort enough, I could have surgery and not even know, but I reserve that kind of excess for special occasions and dire circumstances. Instead, I snarf up tiny rails and get a little lost. The drug stings my sinuses; it feels so bad back there that I sniff up drops of water to clear it out. The slow, fizzy drip of powder, water and snot down my throat tastes the way kerosene smells.

Then? Not oblivion. Just the smooth ride of a wave up and out of myself. It's like I've been half-knocked out of my body. I can see my limbs, make them move, but I don't feel any connection to them. I can feel the keyboard beneath my fingers, but I also can't. My body feels the way static sounds. It hangs, weightless and impossibly heavy at the same time. The drugs and gravity cancel each other out and I am stuck between two planes.

I sink low in my chair in front of my computer and dial into the internet. My modem beeps and wails as it connects. I check my email to see if my ex-boyfriend Will has responded to any of my messages of love and woe: he has not. I do another line and surf some softcore porn sites with distracted interest. Do another line. Log into my preferred online dating sites and browse profiles: see, these are the friends and lovers I could have if I wasn't such a loser. Update my profiles with the latest semi-naked pics I've taken on my shiny new digital camera. If I can get the right combination of images maybe I'll attract the kind of people I'm looking for. I don't know who these people are, but I'll know them when I find them. I cry, dribbling Special K snot onto my top lip, sad but also not that sad. Objectively sad, what with the K. Suck that drug-snot back to make room for another line. And another.

*This is your life.* The thought crosses my mind dispassionately. *This is your life. This is your life and you're obliterating it.* I sure fucking am. I wish I could sleep away tomorrow and tomorrow. I can't, so this is the next best thing. With enough ketamine, who could be lonely? With enough ketamine, who could be properly sad? I'll keep going until I don't have a feeling left, not a pang. I'll keep going until I don't need anybody. I do another line and the feeling intensifies, like I'm standing just to the side of my body and my emotions. Yes, this is what I'm seeking. All my tears dry up. Who needs anything at all, besides drugs? Not me.

Not me.


One night after work, I head to a bar with Zara and another colleague, Sofia. I'm overjoyed. Spending time with people, real live friends! We're weary but looking forward to a drink or two. We settle in, smoking, drinking and talking in the busy pub, perched at a high table in between the bar and the door. It's nice to socialise with them outside of work.

The bar is teeming with people, the air thick and smoky. Out of the haze, a guy approaches us. He's beefy and blond, good looking but none of our types, and he's more than just a little drunk.

'What're youse girls drinking?'

'Hey mate, we're not interested,' Sofia says gently. 'We're just trying to have a chat.' She shuts him down before he even gets started.

'Righty-o, then,' he says, and backs away.

We are in no mood for men tonight. We've had a busy shift at work and we just wanna chug some beers. We go back to telling stories of the clients and the women at work, but not ten minutes later, he's back.

'Can I just say you girls look great tonight,' he slurs, leaning over onto my chair and getting all in my space.

'Mate, we're not interested,' Zara says.

'I'm just trying to be friendly,' he says, not very friendly at all, but he recedes back into the bar.

'Try taking no for an answer,' I say.

Minutes later, he's back.

'So, you're not interested, hey?' he says, then grabs Zara's full beer, lifts it up and pours the entire thing over her head.

I've never seen someone react so fast. Zara fumbles, blind with beer and rage, for the big glass ashtray. Butts fly everywhere as she roars and goes to cork him on the head with it. Sofia and I grab her, holding her tiny frame back, her massive hair deflated with the contents of an entire schooner, the amber liquid dripping from her eyelashes.

'This top is fucking NEW,' she screams. On the other side

of the table he laughs as she struggles against our grip. 'I'm gonna fucking kill you!'

The bouncers intervene and, after hearing our story, chuck him out of the bar. The staff find a bunch of bar towels for Zara to dry herself with. They freshen her drink for free and bring us a new ashtray. Zara takes a sip of her drink, lights up a cigarette, and even with her mane of hair dampened and streaks of beer all over her new top, I've never seen anyone look so poised.

'This top was fucking new,' she says, and shakes her head.


Rosanna is my age – twenty – but she looks about fifteen, like me. I develop a crush on her the instant I see her. She's tiny, blonde-haired and sweet, with bookish glasses and creamy pink cheeks. She's impressively aloof, wears sweet little pastel ensembles and fancy face powder. She is, sadly, not into girls, and definitely not into fuck-ups like me. We do become friends, though. She has a flashy apartment in the inner west and when I go over, I smoke furiously out on her balcony while she watches from inside, amongst her stainless-steel appliances and shiny computer set-up. She does not smoke, does not do drugs.

She seems incredibly grown-up, but together we commiserate on looking so young in this industry. It's so fucked up but just so *usual*. From the way one client talks to me throughout his massage, I get the distinct impression that he is grooming me, and that he's used this tactic before. I reason that it's better the creepy older dudes come and see me than enact their underage fantasies with real teens, but I don't interrogate this further for many years. Why do I accept that some men just get to have fantasies that are legitimately fucked up? And why do I feel like sex workers should have to bear the brunt of these fantasies? Internalised whorephobia is real, and it's *messed up*.

Some guys, even the ones who aren't seeing me because I am young-looking, just make me feel dirty. I spend extra time in the shower after seeing them, trying to scrub the feeling away. It's not what they say, it's how they say it. It's their tone and inflection, the look in their eyes.

Some men get off on making women uncomfortable.

They're seeking that creeping feeling I get when they use a particular phrase or touch a certain way. They want to see me feel it, see the dart in my eyes as I wish the time to leap forward and for this all to be over. I have a great gut. I can tell if I'm safe or not by the churn in my viscera. But I'm not always in the position to turn down bookings. To have every fibre of my being screaming *get away*, *get away*, but still have to feign intimacy? It requires a special kind of compartmentalisation. I take those feelings, box them up and bury them for an hour or so. It's not easy to fight my gut, but I do it, in the name of a buck.

Is it wrong that sometimes I dissociate during bookings? *It's only sometimes*, I tell myself. Just for the bad ones. I'm guilty of often going through my shopping list, planning what I'm going to spend this money on, while I'm sliding all over some strange man. But when a guy sets off my gut, and I have to quash my natural urge to get as far away from him as possible, sometimes it seems as though I'm not there, or like I'm watching myself from above.

It's only sometimes, though. Right?


'Do you know who that guy is?' Grace asks me as I prepare to head into a booking, touching up my lipstick as the client showers.

'No, who is he?' I ask, bent towards the mirror, smacking the red across my lips.

'He's a famous footballer.' She tells me his name.

'I thought he looked familiar!' The only time I see footballers is on the news if I am randomly paying attention to the television that drones in my apartment 24/7 to keep me company. I've seen this guy on the news many times.

He's well-muscled and has a neck like a keg. He's so much taller than me that when I rub up against him, I feel as if I'm preparing to climb a mountain. He barely fits on the table, huge feet dangling off the end. I oil up and climb aboard, revelling in how tiny I am in comparison to his huge frame.

I'll admit it, sometimes I get quite turned on during a booking, and this is one of those times. There's something about his height, his strength, that makes me go over all starry-eyed. I have a bizarre desire to have him pick me up and put me places, like I'm a doll.

*A doll.*

Recognising him from the telly isn't even the biggest part of it. I'm only a baby feminist, but it still feels wrong to go to pieces over feeling small and potentially powerless. Really, I'm the one with the power. I am not afraid of this giant man. I'm cocooned safe inside my parlour with four other girls and a receptionist who'll come running, brandishing stilettos (the shoes, not the knives) if I so much as make a peep out of the ordinary. I'm free to bathe in this feeling, this binary of being powerless/powerful.

And I know who *he* is. He doesn't know me. Anonymity is a power in itself.

One time, another well-known athlete comes in, coked out of his brains, and chases me around the room for two hours, saying, '*CanIeatyourpussy, canIeatyourpussy*?' as I try to get him to calm down and lie down so I can do my job. Once the time is up, he asks to extend the booking another two hours, to which I reply, desperately, 'Hmm, no, I think I have another booking.'

I do not have another booking, in fact business is slow as all hell, but no amount of money is worth another two hours with him. He's short and powerfully muscular, but I'm not afraid he's going to hurt me. He's just a lot to control.

He doesn't even share his coke with me, the greedy bastard.


I go through bongs like most women go through stockings. Ceramic, glass, plastic. I have complex glass creations, ceramic dolphins that require you to smoke out of the tail, sturdy translucent plastic forms. I break them all. Being incredibly clumsy, and always stoned, I inevitably knock them over and smash them on my parquet floors, sending filthy bong water to seep between the gaps in the floorboards. The guy at the sex shop up the road knows me on sight, I'm in so often replacing my bongs.

Leo used to call them my 'dummys'.

Fuck him, but he's right. Once, when we were living together, he threw a hundred-dollar note at me during one of my weed-lacking freak-outs and said, 'Just go and buy it, I can't stand you behaving like this.' I felt useless and pathetic at his words, and they echoed around my head for months, deepening the sense that I am built wrong somehow. Deepening the way that I hate myself.

Luckily, I live on my own now, and the only one who sees me when I run out of pot and become hysterical and pathetic is me.

I try to never run out.

Sometimes, on a good day (or a bad one), I smoke upwards of fifty cones. If I'm home, I can't go more than half an hour without a pull on my bong. Even when my grandparents come to visit, five minutes before they knock on my door, I'm hanging out my window, punching a sneaky last one before they arrive. My house reeks of pot smoke and incense, but I live in the kind of apartment block where most of the units smell this way, so it's not a problem.

I enjoy the ritual of drugs, sure. I love mixing out the right amount of weed and tobacco, doing the quick motion with the scissors, *snip, snip, snip.* Turning the sticky little buds into dust. Packing the piece just right, then shot-putting the smoke into my lungs, the dual punch of tobacco and cannabis. Leaning back and watching the stream of blue smoke as I exhale. The soft fuzz that descends immediately, the lowering of the eyes and upturn of my lips into a blissful smile. The same as I love racking up a rail of speed or coke, measuring out little bumps of K onto my keys, mixing up a shot. There's familiarity there, the busywork of drugs. The difference with cannabis is that it's quantity, as well as quality. I can make a gram of bad coke disappear in a night, the good K is very expensive and speed is grotty bathtub drugs. Weed is always around, always plentiful, cheap and fucking cheerful and effective at blowing my mind, if I smoke it all the time. And I do.

Shelly at Boutique is as big a stoner as I am. She drives me home after our day shifts together. She's such a massive pothead that she takes her bong everywhere with her, which I would probably do if I wasn't reliant on public transport. She keeps it in the footwell of her car, heads out every hour or so at work and punches a few. On our drives home, when stuck in traffic, she ducks down and pulls cones. A truck driver's passenger gives her a grin after he sees her crouching behind the wheel, sucking on her bong. She blows the smoke up at him, the driver sounds his horn twice and his friend gives us the thumbs up. I'm all for it – a lift home and free weed? Yes, please! We become loose friends because of our shared interest in getting blasted.

I have a lot of weed friends. They are people I have very little in common with beyond a shared love of being stoned all the time. My downstairs neighbour is a weed friend. The guy from the cafe who comes and smokes with me, bringing tiny wrapped foil grams he picks up on his way over. Various other stoner babes from work who drop by for a cheeky cone or two after a shift, they are friends but not friends, transient relationships based on a shared need for oblivion.

For a five-or-so month period I only smoke bucket bongs, those epic feats of gravity-assisted weed consumption. I can slam ten buckets in a night, easy. I bring friends over and say, 'Go on, try a bucket.' They try and inevitably cough their guts up, green out and/or vomit. I am so used to punching buckets that to me they seem like no big deal.

See, I'm trying to kill all my feelings, which are too much, and my personality, which is *far too much*. I'm sure smack would work better, but who has time for that? I've got a weird self-preservation instinct that holds me right on the edge of things, and it keeps me away from heroin. I know myself too well. I'd die. Instead I punch cone after cone, dulling myself down to the bare minimum of a person. After a while it just makes me feel normal, and without it my brain is screaming. I think that's why I took to cannabis in the first place. It was the first thing that stopped my brain and its endless chatter and wail. It fills something in me that is missing. I can hold one thought in my brain at a time. Sometimes, no thoughts. Peace. But the lack of it turns the low-level chatter and moan in my brain to a guttural howl.

*You must have it, you must.*

I cannot be alone with myself.

I get a new boyfriend, Jonathan. It just kind of happens.

I'm at my bathroom mirror, smearing my cheeks with foundation with my friend Shakira, an epic beauty and dirty punk I met at Indulge, looking over my shoulder. Shakira is tall and long-haired and fucked up. I adore her. She doesn't know what I'm really like yet, so she's still my friend. My apartment pulses slowly, lights thrumming from the pill she pressed onto my tongue earlier. When we're ready, we thunder down the stairs in our big platform shoes.

The night streets are black and shiny with rain. Redfern station beckons ahead, floodlit, and we go all the way down the long escalator to platform eleven. We whisper, tight-jawed and gently paranoid, on the train until our stop, then pop out at Kings Cross. Our drugs are safely stowed (each in our own body's 'special pocket'), but we hurry past the cops and dogs patrolling the station in the harsh fluorescent lights at street level. Strip club bouncers caterwaul to us, and I drag Shakira past as she ruminates on whether she should start stripping or not.

The building shakes with noise as we approach. I open the door and I'm assaulted by distorted guitars and heavy bass. The club plays a mix of heavy rock, industrial and nu-metal, the perfect accompaniment to a nose-load of speed and a bad attitude. It attracts the kind of rail-thin, drug-fucked, black-clad jerks I'm the most sexually attracted to.

In the bathroom, re-upping our doses, Shakira does a line as she perches on the toilet, then passes me the rolled-up tenner.

'That arsehole I went home with last week is here tonight. Don't let me fuck him again.'

'I'll try,' I tell her, and I lean into the stainless-steel toilet-roll holder and hoover up two lines. My nose is in such poor form from snorting speed all day, raw and blocked, that half the off-white powder just falls out of my left nostril and onto my black mesh top.

'Fuck!' What a waste.

On the dance floor we strobe with the lights, and through the dim I see something I want. When I get closer, I see he has kind eyes and when I yell into his ear and he into mine, I find that he's a gentle Swede. I leave Shakira without saying a word and take him home, spend hours with him in my bed, exploring the sharp planes of his hipbones, the jut of his ribs. As the sun comes up, he leaves me, flushed and satisfied. There's no need for him to see the hideous conclusion to my night. I remain soft-lit and perfect in his memory. For once.

Anyway, this is not my new boyfriend.

I'm almost drifting off to sleep when my phone buzzes. It's Shakira. She's with some friends, can she bring them over to keep the party going? They have drugs! I tell her, 'Of course,' and they roll in, stomping hard on my wooden floors, no doubt waking up the downstairs neighbours. It's Shakira, a guy who I find out is a schoolteacher who has a bunch of coke, and a sweet, laconic lad called Jonathan. We yell back and forth at each other in the manner of people on a lot of cocaine, then Shakira and the schoolteacher retire to the bed to make out, which is kind of awkward in the single room of my studio apartment. Jonathan and I eye each other.

'Wanna … ?' he asks.

'Yeah, okay.'

That's how I meet Jonathan. He's a soft-spoken Samoan labourer, with fine-muscled brown arms and exquisite dark eyes. He stays for two days and we fuck and talk and eat and then fuck again. He's beautiful, quiet, and loves to punch bongs as much as I do. In the next few weeks I text all of my fuck buddies and let them know I'm off the market for a while.

I choose him.

I tell Jonathan about my job that first morning. He just nods. I can tell he's not comfortable with it, and it's better that we don't talk about it. So we don't. He spends weekends at my apartment, smoking bowls, getting takeaways and watching movies. He's so quiet and I'm so talkative that I ramble to fill the spaces between us. I never go to his house, because he still lives with his parents. We always crowd my little studio apartment, falling into bed because there's nowhere else to go. There's not a lot to our relationship. Occasionally we take ecstasy together and he talks with the same fervour I usually do. He opens up, tells me how it really weirds him out, what I do.

'Do you want to pay my bills then, or pay for all this weed?' *Because* I *pay for all the drugs we smoke*, I think but don't say. I reckon he hears it anyway, and he looks hurt.

'It's just—'

'It's my job,' I say. I am indignant. How do I get it across that, when I'm at work, all that sexual stuff I do isn't motivated by the same desires that motivate my sexual advances towards him, that it's a different kind of thing? That the intimacy I conjure at work is both fake and yet real at the same time?

How do I express it in simple words? I can't. He just won't get it. I barely get it. Instead, I do what I always do when I hurt – I punch another cone, trying to haze the pain away.

'It's just a job, like any other kind.'

'No, it's really not.'

*Fuck you*, I think, but don't say. I reckon he hears it anyway.

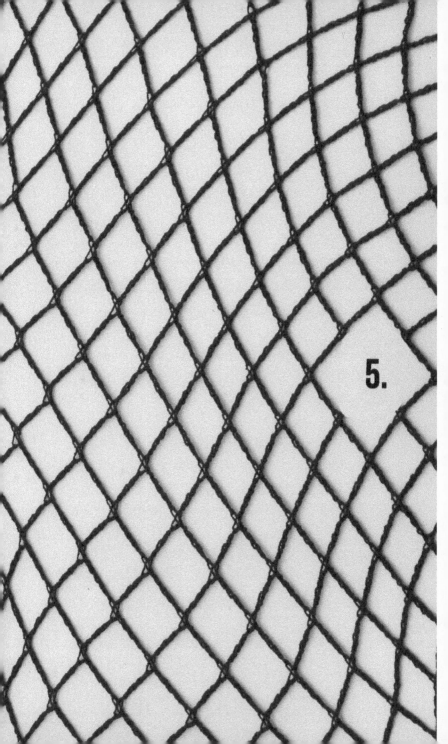

When you're new at a parlour, you're fresh flesh, and inevitably busy. After a while, though, things start to die off unless you reveal yourself to be a perfect ten or a good hustler. I am most definitely *not* a ten. I'm a five, maybe? I'm not sure. It's hard to rate myself. I'm cute, with great tits, but I'm too odd-looking and weird, personality-wise, to be a ten. I have some regulars, but not many. I can't hustle, am not a workaholic and my crazy grates along the inside of me, making a jangly dissonance that the clients can sense. On a good day I can ease the scraping of my moods and I leave with fistfuls of fifties, but I have mostly bad days, head-wise, so this is not a common occurrence.

When your work gets quiet it affects things in a multitude of ways.

The main one is financial, of course. This is my only job and I'm such a disaster with money that I never prepare for the quiet times. When I'm flush, I walk down King Street or through Pitt Street Mall with a fistful of cash, needing to spend it on anything. There are the drugs, of course, which are expensive. It's tough on the wallet to be high most of the time. I start to run out of weed now and then, because my cleaning fee from Dan only covers about half of the drugs I need to smoke, and the hysteria that accompanies the shortfall just makes matters worse. After shopping and buying cigarettes and drugs, there are the other expenses: rent, bills, etc. I have no credit for my phone. I get behind on the rent. I have to pay my bus fare to work in silver coins, a humiliating exercise as the bus driver counts out the change while we idle at the kerb.

Then there's the constant rejection to deal with as well. It's different to being dismissed by a serial rejector – those guys were never going to stay with anyone. But when they're legitimate customers and they consistently choose women who are not me, I start to wonder what the fuck is wrong with me. I'm putting myself out there, prepared to do this thing for the money and nobody's fucking taking. The misery builds as I sit in the staff lounge, jumping at every doorbell, and inevitably getting knocked back. My colleagues bustle from job to job – I distractedly watch cable and nick outside to chain-smoke and seethe. I resort to desperate acts, changing clothes obsessively to see if it's my outfit causing the problem. Yes, it must be the clothes. This dress is not right, if I pair this one with this bra, and change my lipstick, then I'll be flat out.

It is not the clothes.

Clients seem to sense when you need money, and they disappear at the merest whiff of desperation. This only serves to compound my crazy. It's the most vicious of cycles: make no money, stress out, become internally hysterical, try to fix the mask on but it won't fit, make less money. The stakes are higher now I'm living on my own; there's no one to make up the shortfall if I'm having a bad time. Oftentimes I am on the phone to my parents, crying and begging for a loan, but they don't have much themselves and can only help me so much when my life is constantly teetering on the edge of things.

I keep making the same mistakes over and over.

One of the receptionists at Boutique is a beautiful brunette called Tilly. She's a fine receptionist but she and I don't really get along. I've got this feeling she can see the real me, and she hates me, just like everyone would if they knew what I was really like.

I'm in the middle of one of my slow freak-out days about six months into my employ at Boutique. I'm helping out with laundry, as we workers are supposed to when we aren't busy. I learn to fold towels expertly and arrange them into the fancy patterns that each parlour prefers on their tables. I'm in one of the rooms folding the towel just so when Tilly walks in to restock the massage oil. I take the opportunity to moan about how quiet I am, not because I believe Tilly will have any commiserations for me, but because I simply cannot help myself. The words and worry tumble out of me like a knocked-over cup every time someone crosses my path.

Tilly laughs. 'At least *I'm* getting paid to be here.'

Things go a bit funny in my head for a moment – something rips through the misery and sparks it into rage like a live wire snapping into water. I don't see red; I see black. I see stars.

I see Tilly's evil bitch-grinning face and I want to punch it. I don't.

Instead I unleash a tirade of epic proportions, of screamed nonsense, picking things up and slamming them down. I make no sense, I barely even feel like I'm saying real words. All I want is for someone, *anyone*, to feel my pain and desperation, and unfortunately it's coming out on entirely the wrong person, who just grins and shakes her head at me. She charges into the office and calls the boss as I continue my rant, as I harangue her through the closed door. When she opens it again, there's such a satisfied look on her face that I finally shut up.

'You're fired. You need to be off the premises in five minutes,' she says.

'Fuck you, Tilly,' I say, and dissolve into a pathetic lump of tears. Throughout so much chaos I have managed to act my best, and now it's all for nothing. I've done it, I've gone and ruined something that was good because I couldn't control my feelings. *This*. This is why I hate myself. This is why I'm trying to kill my emotions. Because when I let them out, when I let myself feel how I truly feel, they explode out of me with a rage so dazzling and violent that no one can handle it.

'Pack your shit, Sasha. Get out of here.'

There's nothing for it but to cry hysterically as I empty my locker and pack shoes, massage-oil-reeking dresses and lacy underthings into a plastic bag under the haughty and watchful eye of Tilly and the rest of the women, who are all stark silent, soaking up this latest bit of drama for their gossip files. My mascara is running in soft grey rivulets down my blushed cheeks, and I'm smearing red lipstick everywhere. I gently sob and mumble, 'Fuck you, Tilly,' as I carry my assorted shit out of the front door, drop half of it down the stairs. My crying reaches a fever pitch as I try to sweep up my bras and dresses from the stairwell.

I have just enough change for the bus home, so I sit up the back with my arms wrapped tight around my stuff, trying to wipe the mascara tracks off my face and stop crying so I can pass as a normal person on this full bus. People try not to look at me as I gently weep. Ah, there's nothing quite like a mysterious, heavily made-up girl crying in public. I try to stop, but I can't. I cry the whole way home as people's eyes slide past me, and back again.

How many more jobs can I lose because of my mental

illness? Why can't I just be a normal person, with emotions that fall into a manageable range without swinging to such extremes? Why does everything ache so hard, sting so swiftly and sharp that it splits me open like this in front of people? Why can't I keep my fucking mouth shut and lose my shit in the privacy of my own home, like everyone else does?

I really *liked* this job. Boutique is a nice place, with good pay, and Zara is there, a human calmative to my jangled nerves. Now? I've gone and fucked it up.

Again.

After I'm done crying and punching as many bongs as I can, I walk to the corner store and get the paper. I flip past the news and the sports, right to the back where the classifieds are.

It's time to find a new job. Well, a new place to do the old job.

I pour over the ads for parlours, the text the same as those cut-outs I plastered to my school folders only two years before. I pick the ones with the biggest, fanciest ads, knowing that the more money a parlour spends on advertising, the more likely they have good rates and a nice premises.

I start with Madison's, because I am intrigued. Madison's is spoken about as if it's the weirdest massage parlour on earth. And it is.

Imagine that you live in a nice, normal apartment block, then imagine that one floor of this block is a series of studio apartments that serves as a single massage parlour. That's Madison's. It's fucking strange and all the people I come across in the lobby and elevator give me the eye, wondering if I'm one of 'those girls'.

Oh, I am.

On my first day I take the lift up to the designated floor and get my key. The first apartment is an office, where the receptionists run things and the clients approach to find out which rooms have real live girls in them, free for an hour of various rubbing and assorted tugging. I'm allocated a room for the duration of my shift, and I find the right door and head inside. There's an armchair and a massage table and a small bathroom off to the side, a cupboard with many towels, a laundry hamper and a television with no cable. I'm glad I brought a book.

The day is filled sporadically with men knocking on my door. I open, give my spiel and then they head off to meet the rest of the workers. If they like me and want to stay, they pay the receptionist, she buzzes, and I invite them back into my tiny domain for the allocated timeframe.

It's bizarre. And lonely.

I feel cooped up, imprisoned. Like Rapunzel in her tower, with much shorter hair. I smoke out the window with ferocity, one cigarette after another. The best part of working in a parlour is the other women. Cackling in the staff lounge, watching bad cable TV, helping each other with makeup, cuddling or taking valium en masse when it's quiet, telling each other secrets. The clients sometimes feel like an imposition on all the fun we're having. But sex work alone, in this sparsely furnished apartment, is just weird and boring to me. Maybe it's the right kind of place if you're all about the hustle, but I am an otherwise creepy loner who needs to get my social requirements met at work. Madison's is just more of me being alone in my head and that is never a good place for me.

I make it halfway through my book, interrupted by a booking now and then, and at the end of my shift, after collecting my pay, I decide to never come back. Madison's is not for me. I need the candour and the sweep of a girls' room, the chaos of a large number of women being messy and imperfect and beautiful and themselves.

Next, I take some shifts at a place in the city where they roster on far too many women for the number of clients who actually stay. This is a place for hustlers. During intros we line up at the door, a long line of girls snaking up the hallway, and I'm just not the kind of convincing, enthused sex worker who can drum up business in this type of environment. No one is very friendly; it's the kind of atmosphere where everyone is too busy fighting for bookings to do much by way of light banter. I can't cope with it. I need a friendly face, a listening ear, a smoke and a cuppa and camaraderie to do this kind of work.

I find my new place, Exclusive, right beside a massive construction hole that will become a Westfield shopping mall, eventually. It's a big place, set above a row of shops. It is well appointed, and has a bustling, bright staff lounge. The room has a high ceiling, a smokers' lounge adjoining, and is painted a cheery yellow. It is packed with women chatting, hugging, applying makeup. I sink into one of the many couches and wallow in the back and forth between the women working, grateful for the sound and sight of them bonding over dicks and drugs, cosmetics and cock. It's another dress parlour and I feel like a new start, so I buy a brand-new range of skin-tight sheaths, printed gowns and slinky black numbers. I also buy my first pair of Pleasers, strappy and shiny platform heels favoured by strippers for their relative comfort. I delight in practising prancing about in these six-inch monstrosities, but more often than not I just teeter and almost fall.

Exclusive has a selection of rooms ranging from spacious spa rooms to tiny closets, just big enough to get the job done. Every one of these rooms is mirrored to maximum capacity and clients just can't resist getting their grubby fingers all over them. Clean-up is hell, and I feel as though

I spend half my time polishing mirrors, only to have them ruined again with the next booking. It's not sexy to scream, 'Don't touch the fucking mirrors! Jesus!', so I don't, but every misplaced hand and oily palmprint fills me with rage. The place goes through litres of Windex to keep all those mirrors at a high shine, and the receptionists are constantly coming into the staff lounge after bookings to let us know we've missed an errant finger- or arse-print on the wall. Fuck, even the platforms underneath the massage tables are mirrored. Everywhere I look during a booking I can see my oiled body flashing back at me as I work myself across the client. Watching myself give hand-jobs from every mirror is a little disconcerting, and it means I really work on my angles, making sure I look great from all directions, which does sometimes distract me from the task at hand.

The rooms are also *cold*. The aircon is kept at meat-locker temps, and though this puckers the nipples and tautens the flesh, making us workers look great, I'm constantly covered in goose flesh. I cajole the clients into the spa just so I can warm up, and when it comes time for the body-slide part of the booking, I suck up every degree of warmth that I can from their bodies.

Body-sliding involves dexterity – to slowly rub your slippery body over someone as you perch on the edge of a slim massage table, while also avoiding their genitals and avoiding getting *your* genitals on them. Grapeseed massage oil does not agree with vaginal pH, let me tell you. Anyway, all this oiliness leaves you a fucking mess by the end. I'm covered in goop from the oil, from the client. So, I shower after the booking. Thoroughly.

If I'm having a good shift, this could mean showering up to eight times over eight to twelve hours. I don't know about anyone else, but scrubbing my skin with anti-bacterial soap eight times a day is not great for me. My skin dries like crumpled tissue paper. I rub it furiously with body lotion, trying to break even somewhere in there, but the damage is done. My skin begins to do weird things. I break out in a million tiny chest zits. Sometimes my skin starts to crackle and peel. What can I do? Not shower? Not possible.

Oh, Palmolive soap. The sickly smelling, bright-orange bodywash of choice for massage parlour workers in the early 2000s. It's marketed as specifically anti-bacterial and everyone I work with slathers themselves in it after every booking. The standard soaps provided by the parlours are no-name brands of questionable quality, so it's better to bring your own. I carry a standard 'kit' around the parlours in a zippered makeup bag. What goes in it depends on where I'm working. If it's a no-extras parlour it might include the soap, perhaps some massage oil better for the skin than the stuff management provides, and breath mints. If it is an extras parlour, the kit will also include condoms, which the management most certainly does not provide.

The Palmolive soap has this very particular smell, the sickly combination of artificial fragrance and triclosan, and that smell associates so strongly with my erotic masseuse days that I will never again be able to smell it and not think of showering after bookings. Anyway, I chalk my tortured skin up to an occupational hazard, load my shower puff up with killer anti-bacterial soap, and scrub away.

Working at Exclusive starts off a period of time that I might call stable, if you can call my still often hysterical self 'stable' at any point. I go to work, riding my razor scooter to the station, careening across footpaths and to the parlour. I chat with the girls at work, rub some backs, pull some cock, collect my money and go home. Jonathan comes over in the evenings and we smoke a lot of bongs and watch a lot of movies. I don't really go out. I don't do as many other drugs as I used to. I hide my usage from Jonathan and only indulge in secret: snorting lines of K and speed (a 'horserace') and surfing the internet when he isn't around. If I wasn't also still chronically mentally ill, I would call it stability. Maybe monotony is a better word.

I can't decide if I love it or hate it. I miss *dramatics* but feel almost content in my new quiet life. Almost. Inside, just underneath, I roil and bubble, wanting desperately to overflow at the same time as I want to keep this sweet and standard life going. Work is *fine*. My relationship is *fine* (as long as we don't talk about work). Everything is *fine*. I don't know if I like it.

I want everything to be too much, too often, too *too*. And it's not. I get the distinct flash of the ease with which I could keep this up forever, like normal people do. Work, come home, get stoned, fall asleep watching TV. And repeat.

Things with Jonathan and I are at an impasse. Our relationship is *boring*. We don't talk, we don't ever do anything, we just exist together. It's either let things go on like this or break up, and I can't imagine keeping this up forever. I want madcap scrambles, blind and filthy passion. So, I tell him one day: 'We need to break up.'

'No,' he says.

That's that. We go back to watching movies and smoking bongs.

I try again a few days later. 'I think we need to break up.'

'No,' he says.

It takes two weeks for me to get it through to him. When he realises I'm not kidding, he makes a fist. Is he raising his hand to hit me? What the fuck? Instead of my face, he punches the wall of my apartment, which is brick, breaks his hand and has to take time off from his labouring job. This is my fault, of course.

'You fucking whore.'

Ah, there it is.

I mean, I am a fucking whore, yes, but he doesn't have to throw it at me like that.

We dance like this until he just stops coming over. That's it. I am on my own again, and it is time to get dramatic up in here. I don't have to act like I'm normal any more. I don't need to hide my work or my self-mutilation or my drug use. I can fuck whomever I want with passionate, druggy abandon.

I can be drastically *myself* again.

She shows up for her first shift at Exclusive with two open wounds on her arms, right up near her shoulders. Shameless. She doesn't even try to hide them.

The women at work all whisper, 'Did you see that new girl? The cutter?'

Oh yes, I saw her. And I thought, *Oh, honey, I've been there.* I'm just better at hiding it. Not that I think my Band-Aids fool anyone. There's this sense of propriety though, like I have enough shame to at least try to mask the thin slices I put on my arms, legs, breasts, stomach.

'What's that?' Jonathan asks me when we first get together. He runs his finger over the thin scab on my forearm, the soft skin split a little, just enough to sate whatever it is I'm trying to sate.

'Cat scratch,' I say, and we both know that's a fucking lie, but we both sit in it, neither one of us willing to call the other out. Now that we've broken up, I can do what I want, and sometimes what I want is to commit violence to myself. I don't have anyone who specifically cares about what I do, and what I do to myself, so it's a party.

When I come across another self-mutilator it kindles a special kinship inside me. The thin-or-thick, white-or-red of scar tissue in lines glimpsed under the hem of a skirt, the scabs half-healed on the delicate skin of the inner arm tilted at an angle so as not to be too obvious.

Me and this one, I think: *we know*.

I first took a sharp object to my skin when I was twelve. Sewing needles were my drug of choice back then. *Just see it*, my brain would whisper. *Just see a little blood, and everything will be okay.* First just jabs, enough to let out a bead of red. The hurt was a shock, but a balm at the same time. A little spike was fulfilling for a while, but like any drug, the more you use, the more you need. If I tilted the needle to the side, pushed and pulled, the tip would make a jagged line appear, and maybe some blood would spill down the side. *Run*, my brain would whisper. *We need to see the blood run.*

Breaking open a safety razor came next. The tricky, bendy little sliver-blades made perfect straight lines, not the jaggedy rails I could coax with a needle. When I was fifteen I gathered change to buy packs of old-fashioned men's razor blades from the chemist, little white envelopes of ten that I'd slip into my wallet and that would make me feel safe, knowing they were there in case I needed them. The men and women behind the counter looked at me funny as I stood there in my school uniform, wondering why on earth I needed blades for old-fashioned razor sets, or with disapproving glares if they were savvier.

I never go too deep. Just enough to get the blood running a little. To feel the slip and sting. When I feel it, I breathe out a long breath like relief or desire or both.

A few times I have accidents, though. Once, I press the blade in, misjudge and my arm just *opens*. I know it's a mistake right away. I see bits of myself I'm not sure I want to know about. I hold together the wound for hours till it knits.

The scar it makes, though. That's satisfying.

I like my scars. I like to run my fingers over them. Looking at them makes me feel safe, relieved, and sometimes I just need to see the scar to feel better.

I don't want to kill myself, even though my brain often tells me I do. It's not real though. I do not want to die. Cutting is just a way to quell that thought. A small sacrifice to sate that particular beast. If I keep the blood flowing to the altar, then I won't have to go further. Plus, the pain helps. The classic 'feeling alive' phenomenon: watching myself heal, slowly letting the slice return to normal. It's not a metaphor for my life, because that never gets better, really. It's like wish fulfilment. Sometimes it's even a quell for my rage, a way to snap back to myself when the anger gets too much; a shock to bring me back into my body from the stratosphere of fury. And sometimes it stands as a tribute to my self-contempt. This is all you deserve: blood and pain and scars.

It's so many things at once, this need. It fulfils so many different desires. That's why I don't stop.

I make room for the new girl, the cutter, on the couch next to me. She sits down.

'I'm Sasha,' I say.

'Charlie,' she says back.

'How are you?' I ask, friendly.

'Good, yeah,' she says, bright.

We both know that's a lie. But with fresh wounds like that, hers open to the air and mine hidden under strips of plastic, it's kinda true as well.


John is a client I've seen on and off for a while. Wherever I'm working, he inevitably finds me. He goes *everywhere*.

John's different. I like him. He's gentle, soft, and the massage routine isn't the main focus. His bookings are easy and fun. What he likes is introducing new people to his fantasy. It's incredibly specific, and not for everyone. He finds people who are into the idea, and he sees them for a while. He delights in the fact that I love his fantasy, and he becomes a regular of mine.

See, what John wants is to not have balls any more. No testes. Zip.

He tells me this the first time we meet, half gleeful, half ashamed. I get it. I wouldn't want to have balls either. I love indulging John's fantasy. It breaks up the monotony of the standard rub-slip-slide-tug of massage. I whisper to him about cutting his balls off, what I'll do with them (into a jar on my shelf) once the deed is done. He tells me all about what drew him to this specific fetish and I find it fascinating. I love learning all the ins and outs of what makes someone focus in on a particular fantasy, search it out and repeat it. I tie tight strings and ribbons around the offending articles, yank on them hard. It makes me feel powerful, and this is something that I actually like to feel. I could get used to it.

'You're really fascinated by this, aren't you?' he asks me one day.

'Yeah, it's different. And interesting.'

'Have you ever thought about being a Mistress?'

I had. I went for an interview at a dungeon when I was eighteen years old, fresh out of home. I spent an hour talking to the Head Mistress, but I got overwhelmed and ignored my phone when she called me back. I was always a bit intrigued by BDSM. When someone asked me, at seventeen, to piss on them I thought, *Why not? That sounds fun.* I kinda like pain. I have a pair of handcuffs in my bedside drawer that I use frequently.

'Yeah, maybe.'

'I go to The Manor.'

'The dungeon?'

'Yes. You should come with me one day.'

'Yeah, sure.' Clients sometimes push the 'meeting outside of work' thing. I'm not into it. But John, he seems so harmless. When he asks me for the third time if I want to go to The Manor, this time for my birthday, I decide, *Why not? It sounds like fun.*

'Go on then, make the booking,' I tell him. John picks me up in his little sports car on my birthday and drives me to a pair of normal-looking terraced houses in the inner city. We wait on the front doorstep as the bell chimes dimly inside, and then a neat-looking older woman lets us in and shows us into the waiting room. It's spacious and carpeted in soft, plush carpet, with a leather chesterfield that I perch on, nervous. After a while the Mistress that John has booked comes through. Her name is Marceline. She's tall and long-limbed with a kind face, a platinum blonde wig and spectacular PVC outfit. She discusses the terms off to the side in whispers with John. It's my birthday surprise, after all. She does get my consent for a few basic activities but leaves things vague. Then she directs us to the bathroom where John and I shower in quick succession and wait, towel-wrapped, for Marceline to return. When she does, she leads us downstairs to the dungeon and it begins.

We don't indulge John's castration fantasy this time, as the booking is really for me. Marceline spanks me, softly at first, then harder as my arse warms up and turns pink, then red. She flogs me with a soft suede flogger, and I relax into the soothing breeze it makes, the gentle thud of it on my back and bum. Then she ties me to the St Andrew's cross on the wall. As John watches gleefully, she brings over a sterile tray: clamps, jewellery, needle. She's going to pierce my nipple! I'd lost my right piercing a while ago and had complained to John about only having one, so this is his gift to me.

Marceline clamps my nipple, teases it with her gloved finger. Then she brandishes the needle and pushes it through my nipple in a quick, shocking movement. It hurts so much but is over in a second. She follows the jewellery through as she removes the needle, then unclamps my nipple. As the blood rushes back into the area, a runner spills down my chest. This is so different from the blood I spill myself. This hurt is different. It comes from a place of care. Marceline and John can see the beauty in my pain and blood. It's the kind of tending to that I crave, and sure, it might seem like a weird way to get it.

Things go a bit woozy for a moment, what with the shock of the piercing, so Marceline quickly unties me, and John carries me over to the bench, where they both gently caress me, telling me I'm brave and beautiful until I feel better.

I like the entire experience, but this is the part I like the best: the bit where they take care of me after.

\* \* \*

Exclusive has a top earner, a perfect ten, as well. Of course it does; all parlours do. Her name is Jessa and I never quite get a handle on her. She's enigmatic, mysterious. She spends most of her time in bookings and not running her mouth in the staff lounge like the rest of us do. She's a trained masseuse and combines this with the sensual aspect of the service in a way that makes the clients go wild. She has a stable of regulars who book her to the maximum parameters of her shifts. She makes fucking bank, and she's frugal in the way that a lot of top earners are. She hints at owning real estate. She's using this work to set herself up for the future.

She's no bombshell, but she's gorgeous in her own special way. She's a haughty-looking woman with thatches of dark hair under her arms, which kind of drives me a little wild whenever I catch glimpses of it. She's stand-offish though. Guarded. I ache to know more about her. I miss Zara, the perfect ten who tried to try to share her secrets with me, even though it didn't help. Now that we don't work together, I don't see her as much.

I'd love to be a top earner, but with my fractured boundaries, low self-esteem and wildly swinging moods, I simply don't have the tools to be able to soar as high as they do, and there's no way I can fake it. My mood is plastered all over my face, bright as a bloody handprint on a white wall. Clients can smell unchecked mental illness even if you're good at hiding it, which I am not, just like they can smell desperation for money.

Anyway, I don't think it's something you can learn; it is simply something that you *are*, an intrinsic skill like singing or having an artistic eye. But what would it be like, to be so appealing to men that they throw heaping piles of money down to spend an hour with you? That fascinates me. It makes me jealous.

See, I wrap a whole lot up in how men see me, and specifically, if men want to fuck me. I mean, I don't always want to fuck them, which is why erotic massage is such an ideal profession for me, because I don't *have* to fuck them. Just knowing that they want to fuck me is enough.

It satisfies something inside me, something that's missing, that I've never had, or maybe had once but lost somehow. I barely remember a time before the sweeping need pulled on my veins, that need for men's attention. It's embarrassing how much I need it, and when I'm seeking it it's so blisteringly obvious that I surge with shame at the thought of anyone I know observing me. I know these feelings are misguided. The first strings of feminism are just unfurling inside me, and I focus on this desire as another thing that's wrong with me. Real women don't ache and roil with need for men to notice them, do they?

Jessa has the undivided attention of many men.

You bet I'm fucking jealous.

That and the money. I could use a bit of that too.

When I break up with Jonathan I embark on an epic fuck-fest with a grand parade of strangers and friends.

I have this gift, see.

I walk into a club, usually a ratty one in the Cross or on William Street, that plays heavy rock, goth or metal. I light a cigarette because we can still smoke in clubs, and I let my eyes wander over the crowd.

I'll know them when I see them.

There they are. Usually they are men, because my gaydar is untuned and I can barely ever tell when a girl is into me. Women are so much harder to finesse; men are easier for me. *There.* That is the one I will take home tonight.

And I always do. I get who I want. I enter the club, pick my game and hunt. I need sex and attention like I need air.

You could argue, and many have, that it's easy for a woman to pick up random dudes for sex.

I know. I'm so glad it works in my favour.

I come across the gentle Swede, who I also slept with the night I met Jonathan, working behind the bar at my favourite club. He pours me free drinks all night, but I don't go home with him. His plan backfires when I get so drunk

123

that I start making out with a pretty, bald metalhead. I keep looking at his face and wondering what is missing. Eyebrows, that's it! The Swedish punk gazes after me, sad, as I lead No Eyebrows up the stairs and back to his place, where his roommate is so happy he's brought someone home that he doesn't even mind the noises coming from the bedroom. I leave in the early morning, abandoning my best bra somewhere in his messy room. It's a small price to pay to not have to wake him up.

Fucking strangers is my favourite. The discovery of a new body, a new set of features, the excitement that comes from the first time. Sex for me is always good. I've never tied my own pleasure to someone else. I know how to manipulate my body to the things it likes. I'm not afraid to instruct. I know how to get what I want. Strangers are my favourite, but I also have a rotation of five or so guys who I can call at any time and summon to my bedroom to lose a few hours or days.

Sex is a drive, a need, and I will go to great lengths to get it. Catch trains and buses across the city, pay for taxis to deliver the willing supplicant to my door, make the cover charge for clubs up out of coins so I can prowl.

After sex one night, a friend tells me I would be into his friend, then calls and arranges a meet-up for me. I've got my fuck buddies procuring me more fuck buddies. I spend sweaty afternoons with a drummer whose hard body and strong arms wrap tight around my body and my neck until I can barely breathe, the feeling sexy and dangerous. I meet a girl at work who takes me home and watches me intently as I fuck her boyfriend, reaching out now and then to caress my face, my breasts. My ex-boyfriend Will, my first: we taught each other to be filthy years ago, and now we spend days in bed, fucking until we are so sore we actually cannot continue.

I like sex. A lot of it, and crazy sex too. Of course I do! I wouldn't have this drive if I didn't. But it's so very complicated. Sometimes it is another form of self-destruction on top of all the other ways I love to self-destruct. It's a way to get people to spend time with me, because I can't imagine any other reason for them to do so. It's exactly as much attention as I need. Being slutty isn't self-harm for everyone, but it sometimes is for me. It's a drug. It's just another way to make my brain shut up. It makes me feel embodied when I otherwise feel like a big, crazy head on a stick, a balloon on a string tugging in the wind, threatening to fly away. Pinned to the mattress, someone above and around and inside me, I can feel my body.

*You are here, you are real, you exist.*

6.

I'm great at burning bridges. This is evident in my calamitous departure from Boutique, but I don't always get fired for my bad behaviour. Instead, there are times when I embarrass myself so fully and utterly that I quit in mortification instead.

I act out in infinite variations. It can be quiet and sadly unobtrusive: I simply cry for no reason, or for all of them, no matter who I'm in front of or where I am. I ribbon my arms or thighs with cuts, not caring enough about who might see them, and providing no explanation, leaving them to deal with my silent display. Sometimes there's firework-explosion dramatics! Maybe I go hard on the drugs, teetering right on the edge of too-many, too-much, slurring and flopping about. Or I could unleash on my closest peer, proximity-wise, a great flow of stream-of-hysterical-consciousness right in their face.

Mostly, though, it's in the middle. A combination of the above where I vent my misery and pain to anyone who'll listen in great gluts of words that pour out like I'm a tap on full bore.

My departure from Exclusive is the result of one of these actings-out. Or many. It's an old story for me: I'm not making much money, I'm running out of drugs, my rent is overdue, my phone's out of credit, and I can't stop telling *everyone*. People get this look in their eyes when I'm on a misery rant, like *Please get me out of here*, and I can see it, but I cannot stop. This day, a Tuesday like many before, I arrive at work having spent the last of my cash on cigarettes and my train fare, and I'm desperately sad and desperate to tell someone, anyone, about it. As the day jags on and the bookings don't happen, things get out of hand. I'm blubbering in the staff lounge, chain-smoking and venting to anyone who'll listen about my many, many problems.

'... and if I don't get a booking soon I'm gonna have to jump the train home, and the last time that happened I got caught and fined and I just can't believe it's so quiet today, and it's not fair and I'm almost out of smokes again, fuck, and ...'

The manager, a poised blonde woman called Amanda in sensible heels and a smooth black pantsuit, walks in after hearing about my tearful monologue from the other women. She asks me to come with her. She takes me to one of the more spacious massage rooms and invites me to sit.

Is she about to fire me? Fuck! Not again.

'Sasha,' she says, like a sigh, like the thought of my name makes her just so tired that she can barely summon the words. 'You can't come in to work and cry all day.'

'I know, I'm sorry,' I say. 'It's just that I haven't been getting many bookings lately, and I have no money and I'm a little bit upset about it and ...'

'I understand,' she says, sensing that I'm building up and cutting me off before I can. 'But you're making the other girls uncomfortable. You can't act like this in front of everyone. They're all really worried.'

'I'm sorry,' I say. The shame rinses through me. What have I done? I am mortified.

'Here,' she says. She hands me a twenty-dollar note. 'Take this and go home. Come back tomorrow when you're feeling better.' The way she looks at me as she hands me the note is both exasperated and pitying. I don't doubt that this has come out of her own wallet, and that she's showing me what is probably a reluctant kindness, and I feel utterly disgusted with myself. I take the note and dry my eyes, because the misery is fast evaporating and being replaced with a flood of humiliation. Everyone offers mumbles of sympathy as I pack my things and I just nod, wide-eyed and blank, holding in screams of rage at myself.

The next day, after an epic and bloody night spent punishing myself for my public misery display, I call Exclusive. Thankfully, Amanda does not answer the call. I cancel my

131

upcoming shifts and lie that I'll let them know when I'm coming back.

I'm never going back. I can't. I'm too mortified to ever set foot in that place again.

Years later I will see Amanda on the street, waiting to cross at an intersection, and the shame will curdle my gut, still, even after all that time.

I head back into my favourite sex work factory, Indulge. It's like an old lover; I know the terms. She'll always be busy, always have room for me. I can make money there.

There are familiar faces, and lots of new ones too. There's a never-ending cycle of people who are keen to do this work and make good money. So many that there are hundreds of parlours in Sydney. If anything, there are too many workers, and not quite enough clients. Still, the variety needs to be there; customers like a choice. Even if they know what kind of erotic masseuse they are looking for, without a choice, men would rather stay away. That's why shifts are packed to the rafters with women.

So many people choose to do sex work, for a million different reasons. If you think you don't know anyone who has done this kind of work, think again. You have friends who have done sex work, for sure. Domming, stripping, web-camming, massage, full service. They just haven't told you.

Me, I tell everyone. It's no secret.

Well, except to my family. It doesn't concern my parents and so they don't need to know. Really, there's a lot that I'm doing that they don't need to know about. I reckon the information that I pull dick for money might upset them, make them worry, and I'm *fine*, so I avoid the topic. (Okay, maybe I'm not fine, but my professional hand-jobbing is, like, the least of my problems.) To them, I work in catering. I'm working in an 'events space'. Close enough, right? Events definitely occur in the space I work in. I am *catering*, all right.

I don't have shame about the work, but other people do. The stigma surrounding sex work never fades. The idea that a woman is selling her body when she does sex work pervades. If sex work is the selling of a body, can't the same be said about other forms of bodily labour? Any sort of physical work for compensation could be classified as 'selling a body'.

Sex work is the exchange of a service for money. Everybody does that. Transactional service is the basis of capitalism. I don't like the system, but I don't have any choice but to play.

So, I'll play on my terms.

Anyone might wonder, with my blasé attitude to whom I fuck and my constant desire, why I don't do full-service sex work. The real reason is: I don't know. I'm completely supportive of anyone who does full-service work and will later go on to date a full-service sex worker, but it just doesn't seem like it would be right for me. My desire seems boundless, but it's not. There are strict codes and conduct that stoke it.

Even to me, it seems a waste: I could go to a brothel and make more money, but I just don't want to. I'm happy with giving handies, sitting on faces, and the occasional blow job at the massage parlours.

While I'm fine with anyone doing whatever for an honest buck, some women who do sex work very actively participate in what is known as the 'whorearchy'. Some strippers see massage parlour workers as dirty, some massage parlour women will look down on full-service workers. Some dominatrices see any other kind of hands-on sex work as less than. I've always been open to whoever doing whatever they like, but I do admit that I let peer-gleaned ideals get the better of my attitude in the beginning. '*We're not prostitutes,*' massage women hissed. I mean, we say *sex worker* now, 'prostitute' comes from the latin *prostitut*: 'exposed publicly, offered for sale', which is kinda demeaning, don't you think? And anyway, the whorearchy is bullshit. We're all just trying to make dollars, no matter what part of the sex we are selling.

'Sasha, Jessie, the client in meeting room three wants a double with you.'

A double! Jessie and I look at each other with wide grins and bashful eyes. A double can mean a few different things: the client wants two babes to devote all their attention to him; he wants to see a bit of kissy-touchy softcore girl–girl action; he wants to pay to watch two women fuck. What happens in the booking is mostly up to him and how much money he has, or how comfortable the women are with each other, but sometimes it doesn't matter what the customer wants. Sometimes the two masseuses he picks have been waiting for this moment since they started working together, and the guy could be on Mars for all they know.

This is the case for Jessie and me.

We've worked together at a few different places. She's a curly haired redhead with a tidy smack habit that she's confided to me, though she's in methadone treatment and doing much better now. Her skin is silky and just so slightly freckled, her nose a tiny ski-jump. When we get into the room with the freshly showered client, things don't start slowly. He cannot believe his luck as we dive headlong into each other, her hands sweeping down the sides of me as we kiss.

'Fuck, yeah,' he says, a hand on each of our heads as if he's got any semblance of control over the situation, as though he's the one we're doing this for. We let him think that. The fact that we're in lingerie means that it's easy to get each other out of our clothes. Jessie pushes me back against him and I settle in like he's a flesh recliner I'm sprawled across. She kisses my breasts, my stomach, settles in between my legs.

'Yeah, yeah,' the client says, all his lesbian porno dreams coming true. I wind my fingers through Jessie's strawberry curls, trying to ignore the sharp poke of our customer's cock into my back. Why did we wait so long to do this? Why couldn't I have kissed her of my own volition? Asked her on a date? Why couldn't the first time we had sex be uninterrupted by the lustful encouragement of some random dude? I remember that she has a boyfriend, a longterm kind of thing, so I guess I'm grateful that I have this opportunity.

I like women. I have known I liked women for as long as I've had sexual desire. I'm just terrible at letting them know.

I was out in high school in the nineties, my sexuality revealed accidentally by a friend to the entire school when I was fifteen, which had disastrous consequences for my social standing. I spent a lot of time explicitly making sure my female friends knew I *wasn't* into them. My disinterest had to be demonstrative, or they'd give me the terror-look, like, 'Are you imagining me naked?' I was *not* invited to many sleepovers after that. I was so wrapped up in making sure that girls knew I didn't like them that I don't think I learned much about how to let them know I was interested.

In time the idea of my bisexuality sunk in, and I became

the girl that other girls experimented with. I was *just fine* with this. They approached me, usually emboldened by a few drinks, and I, fear curbed by having had a few drinks myself, would acquiesce. This way, I didn't have to put myself out there, didn't have to risk anything, didn't have to face ridicule or an uppercut.

This is my courtship method of choice: I let my proclivities be known and wait for women to approach me. This means I usually end up with women who are bold and oftentimes dominant. I adore dominant women. I puddle at their forthright touch.

But I usually fuck men. Not because I am more attracted to men, and less attracted to women, but because it is just easier. The 'queer' scene is still a little further off, and I'm just not gay enough for the gay spaces. When I go to gay events and club nights, my bisexuality is met with distrust. I don't want to generalise, this is just *my* experience. I find that the kind of women who are into me are mostly other bisexual women. A lot of the time they are in relationships with men, because, like me, they find it easier to navigate that arena. Most of my sexual encounters with women are illicit hook-ups with partnered women, threesomes alongside their partners, or doubles at work that 'don't count' as infidelity, but hey: I'll take what I can get.

Jessie is bold, the kind of take-charge woman I'm extremely attracted to. Her mouth is clamped between my legs, one hand reaching up to squeeze my breast and the other working its way inside me as our customer whispers, 'Oh my god,' and I try to ignore him. I can't concentrate enough to come with him there, so I motion for Jessie to stop and pull her up so she's perched above my mouth. She faces no such distraction from the client, and she rocks against my tongue until she shudders and collapses.

We get the client off as an afterthought, like 'Oh yeah, that'. He doesn't mind, he thinks he's just been involved in the hottest thing he's ever seen, masturbatory fodder for years to come, when really he was a conduit. He could have been anyone.

Jessie and I shower and dress after the client is gone, then clean the room like after any other booking, except we keep throwing each other little smiles as we dry the shower, lay out the towels just so. Just before we leave she presses me against the door and kisses me and I want to take her again – just us – but the night is busy, bookings await and someone will need the room. She goes out, clicking up off the hallway in her high black heels and I watch her until she disappears into the staff lounge.

A few weeks later Jessie disappears from Indulge, tumbling back out into Sydney's massage parlour glut, but every time I take a booking in that room I think of her.

Indulge's staff lounge is ratty but spacious, with benches around the edges, cushions on the floor and one side banked with lockers. At the back of the space is another small room, with glass windows through to the main room. This is the smoking room. It is a fetid, clouded space crammed with smoking sex workers in various states of undress. It fucking stinks, reeking of fresh smoke and the older, more insidious smell of the discarded butts crammed into the ashtrays. The smoke beats against the glass windows in curls and plumes, then gathers around the ceiling, nowhere else to go.

It's disgusting, and I love it.

I spend half my shifts in there, not caring that the smell permeates everything, my clothes and hair. In that room cigarette smoke is like an atmosphere, and it's the one best suited to my physical needs. I puff and puff and wait for clients so that I can ooze over them, drape my cigarette-reeking hair across their bodies.

I'm in between bookings, puffing on a cheeky cigarette in the hazy smoking room. It's busy this evening and the room is empty but for a few women also between clients. The night has been back to back with punters, and everyone's edgy and charged from the work and the money and the drugs that are no doubt circling, snuck into women's bags or brought in by the clients.

I'm just grinding my cigarette out when there's a screech and a wail. I open the door and step out, peering around.

There, by the lockers. Hallie and Katy. Hallie is a long-haired brunette with creamy skin and French-manicured acrylic nails. Katy's lineage is Brazilian, she's long and lean with smooth brown skin and high-lit hair. For some reason, they are pissed at each other.

'You're a liar,' Hallie spits.

'Shut up, you fucking bitch,' Katy says back.

I have no idea what's happened. Maybe someone sharked the other's client? Did something get stolen? I try to look as unobtrusive as possible, not making any sudden movements, not wanting to incite anything. I'm interested to see where this goes.

Plus, I'm the only witness. That means I've got the sole rights to the gossip which may, nay, *will* be hot property if this goes on any longer.

'You're a fucking liar!' Hallie shrieks. Katy throws down her little bag of supplies and slams into Hallie. A tussle ensues, hands slapping into each other, elbows thrown. Suddenly there's an audible snapping sound. Hallie goes down, blood flowing from the acrylic nail that's been prised up and snapped off her finger. A surge of bile rises in my throat.

Hallie lets out a cry of pain and rage, and then charges at Katy, clutching her hand. By this time someone else has come in and she grabs Hallie, holding her back from Katy, who's babbling a stream of profanities about what a fucking whore Hallie is. Both women are crying; mascara is everywhere.

Katy gets fired; Hallie goes home sniffling with her hand swathed in bandages.

'Oh my god, what happened?' the room choruses as the shift winds down. Everyone looks at each other and then I step into the spotlight, holding my gossip aloft like a trophy.

'Well, it went down like this . . .'

Fights are uncommon in parlours. Women rarely use their fists, or their fingers and an acrylic nail, to sort out their problems. Instead, they bitch behind backs. They backstab. They exclude, they glare and start rumours. It's like high school, but with grown women in lingerie. The drama behind the scenes at a parlour can become just as addictive as the money. There's always something, a scapegoat, low-hanging fruit. At a no-extras parlour, rumours will swirl about workers giving blow jobs on the sly. At an extras parlour, it will be about those blow jobs being given for free. Someone's always in the shit — it keeps things exciting. I've borne the brunt of it at times: the little whispers that I was fucking the boss back at Slide; once I left my journal at a parlour and it went around like wildfire that I was a 'crazy bitch'. It's not just the underliers who cop it. Tall poppy syndrome abounds. Anyone who rises too high is also ripe for gossip. It's a 24/7 drama factory, and if you manage things right, you can get all the intrigue you need at work, leaving your life outside relatively drama-free.

Not for me though. I need constant stimulation, like an

inattentive child. Drama at work, drama at home. I want everything to be too much, too exciting, too *too*.

\* \* \*

'How'd you do?' Julie asks me as we wait in a wobbly little line by the office to be paid at the end of shift. It's late, ten past four in the morning, and it's been reasonably busy. I'm epically tired, with my makeup sliding down my face and my feet sore from hours in heels.

'Yeah, pretty good!' I say, doing the sums in my head. We never talk exact numbers. It's not polite. What if someone's had a shitty night? You don't want to make them feel bad if you've made a killing.

'I could have done better,' Julie says, a little gloomy.

Oh money! I love it. I need it. I hate it.

I love the way it feels when I've got a lot of it, the plasticky slip of notes in my hands. I love to count it, shuffling the bills between my fingers, teaching myself to count like I see other sex workers counting: a hard flick-slide of notes from one hand to the next, perfect for adding up large sums, hard-earned. Sometimes, late at night when I'm feeling particularly lonely or sad and I have enough of it, I count my money over and over, getting the rhythm just right. After good nights at work I waft the notes under my nose, breathing in the smell. Dollars! I admit I've even rolled in a couple of thou once or twice. Why not? I do it just to say I've done it. Come to think of it, that's why I do a lot of things.

Because I've never had any money, I'm not sure what to do with it now. People who grow up broke either become great with money or terrible with it. I am the latter. I try to put a little away, I really do, but I'm always raiding my savings stashes (I like to hide mine in books) to buy weed or pay rent.

The receptionist, who looks just as tired and haggard as Julie and I, adds up our totals and pays us out in crisp bills.

'Here you go, sweetheart, you had a good night,' she says, handing me a little stack of fifties.

I sign on the dotted line to say I've received it and stuff the money into my bra. I've got plans for this cash: paying my overdue rent, scoring a couple of microdots, maybe some new shoes?

It's all spent, already. I never learn.

I squint at the pictures. I don't pay the membership for the meet-up site, so all I get are thumbnails. Even rendered tiny, in grainy black and grey, I can see she's my kind of woman. Dark hair, wicked eyes.

I do another bump of Special K and compose a message. She responds right away.

Her name, she says, is Amie. I've got no idea how much she's going to change everything about my life.

We back and forth for a little while but arrange to meet quickly. I don't like to fuck around with online suitors, I like to get to the real-life stuff.

We meet in public, on the day-bright balcony of a cafe. She drinks coffee, I drink tea, and we both smoke furiously.

'What do you do?' she asks.

'I'm an erotic masseuse.'

'Ha! I work in a brothel!'

It's perfect. She's perfect.

The first time we kiss, the first time we fuck, gets lost in a permanent drug-haze. What sticks from the first few weeks: her teaching me to make coffee so I can bring her cups when she sprains her ankle. The soft daze of kissing her; her smile with the capped front tooth; cigarettes, bongs and lying in bed for days. Sitting in the bath playing checkers. The way I can lose parts of myself in fucking her; the way we fumble into each other for hours; the still, cold air around us as we sleep, afterwards.

I'm besotted.

I don't stop fucking strangers when I meet Amie. We just start doing it together. We use the internet to set up dates, go to clubs and pick up schoolteachers, policemen, tradies. We drop them like flies. We are quite the pair, we make a scene everywhere we go, and I've never been so happy.

The neighbours hate us: our revelries go on into the early hours of the morning, fuelled by lust and drugs. One night, after a particularly vocal interlude, someone from the apartments above us screams, 'Will you fucking bitches shut up?' We do not.

I read her thoughtful, dark stories, and I show her my stupid poems, the ones I've never shown anyone. I revel in the exquisite attention she grants me, sensing my need. I want to be better for her, but I'm so massively flawed that the odds seem insurmountable. I'm afraid that if I tell her how far I'm falling into her, she'll run away scared, but when I do, she doesn't run. In fact, she says it to me first.

'Can I say that I love you without it meaning too much?' she asks.

'Yes,' I lie, because it already does.

She tells me she loves me, packs me another cone.

'I love you too.'

I almost don't like being *this* in love. It tugs at me, a need to be with her, to let her consume me. Love is an emotion, and I'm trying to kill those, remember? I feel out of control and it's terrifying.

In the half-light of her apartment before I leave for work, I compose Amie a shrine to say goodbye for the day: polaroids, pills, notes and poems, cigarettes, syringes. I arrange them carefully with bits of paper, flowers. I don't want to wake her, so I try to say goodbye and tell her I love her with trinkets and symbols.

I set the last piece in place, assess my work, then close

the door slow and soft. I walk out into the cool morning, breath fogging, hands jammed deep in my pockets. I'm on my own, but for the first time in as long as I can remember, I don't feel alone.

\* \* \*

A bunch of the Indulge women and I are sitting on shift and it's slow. It's a weekend, and this is the part of the night where the punters are out, before they come drunk-stumbling in to partake of our services.

'Should we drop a pill?' Cynthia says. She daylights as an ecstasy dealer and she's got ten or so in a bag on her. She pulls it out and shakes it gently, teasing us with the little yellow tablets within.

'Why not?'

'That sounds fun.'

'Yes!' I shout. I hand her twenty bucks, mates rates, before she can even open the bag, and I pop the pill she proffers into my gob, swallowing it down with a slosh of warm Coke. Everyone else displays a little more chill, but soon we're all in that sparkly place as we feel the first tendrils of the drug start to wrap around and warp us. We've got towels laid out on the floor and everyone lies down, clad in lingerie and grinning like motherfuckers. I come back from the bathroom and dive headlong into the pile of women, kicking my legs and squashing my face into their boobs and bellies as they giggle.

'I fucking love youse girls,' I say, the drug starting to peak, as I wriggle in between them. It's not just the drugs; I think I do love them. I think I love almost all the women I've met in parlours. There's just something about the intimacy of being around fellow sex workers that I've never found anywhere else. Now that I've got the sweet song of MDMA playing through my veins, I just *have* to tell them. 'Nah, I'm serious. Youse are some of the best girls I've ever met. I fucking love you.'

'We love you too, Sasha,' they chorus, and I feel the pure joy of acceptance. I'm just so fucking happy, and glad I'm here! I want everyone I know to know, so I start sending out garbled text messages to my friends and lovers, letting them know that I love them too. I'm going to wake up to some confused text messages in the morning, but there's no time to think about that now, this is important. Love!

Someone turns on music and we start to bop along, still lying on the floor. We dance with our hands and feet, eyes closed and smiling massively. We hold hands, and hug, and give each other saucy little closed-lip kisses. *This is why I love drugs*, I think. The kinship I feel right now, I can't get anywhere else. That thought sobers me for a second. Fuck me, I wish I could feel like this every day. Maybe that's what I'm chasing with my drug use. Not killing my feelings at all, but feeling special, feeling kinship, feeling love and feeling as though I can express that love. Why can't I feel like this without drugs? It isn't fair!

One of my exes, during a fight, once said to me: 'You don't know how to love anything.'

They were referencing my mental illness, my obviously disordered personality, saying that it rendered me incapable of love. I don't know if they said it to hurt me. I didn't know then that I would never forget it, that my mind would whisper it to me for years to come, that every time I have a legitimate feeling for someone or about something, I will question myself and doubt my emotions. I'm afraid that it hurts so hard because it's true.

'What on earth is going on in here?' the receptionist says, opening the door and snapping me out of my devastating reverie.

'Nothing!' we chorus from the floor, then collapse into giggles.

'Whatever it is, get over it, we've just had two walk-ins. Intro rooms one and two.' She goes out shaking her head.

'Oh shit!' Cynthia says and we all fall down, giggling again.

'This guy is gonna get the worst fucking massage of his life!' Hallie barks and we laugh again, then straighten our bras, hitch up our G-strings and parade out for the meet in a wobbly, cackling line.


I could stay lost in Amie for days, and I do. I could fuck her until we fall to pieces.

We create a great mess all over the apartment when we make a day of it. Amie is into BDSM, and I like things that are sexy and fun, so the bedroom, lounge room and bathroom all get covered like a fetish bomb has exploded. She ties me down to the coffee table, we hit each other with soft suede floggers and sharp, stingy canes, dress in latex and get in the bath to take photos. It's a way to make sex last for hours, days, and it does. It's playful, dirty and a little bit dangerous, just the way I like things.

The thing with BDSM is you've got to have trust. At first, I trust Amie implicitly, and hand my body and my well-being over to her. And she to me. Once I wrap her entirely in plastic wrap, including her face, leaving only a tiny hole for her mouth. I bind her so tightly and totally that she is completely immobile, depending totally on me. She trusts that I will monitor her breathing. Trusts that I will check on her and make sure she does not overheat. Trusts that I will let her out when the scene is done. Trusts that I will care for her.

When I sub for Amie and she hands me back to myself in one quivering piece, whole, the feeling is revelatory. Seeing that love is care, with barriers that will not be broken. She will take me down this path, but only as far as I can handle, and when I say so it will stop.

This place doesn't have a stupid name; it's just an address: 74 Abernathy Street. A fellow worker runs it, a neat little blonde called Aubrey. Her paypig, a regular client who finances her life and endeavours, gives her the money to set up the parlour. I take some shifts there to help out. It's closer to home than all the other places, and Aubrey gives me the day shifts, so I don't have to worry about spending any of my earnings on a taxi home. I ride my bike in and haul it through the front rooms so no one busts the lock and steals it.

The parlour is a converted terrace house with tiny showers installed in every room. Everything is unused, the towels still slippery in the way that new towels are. The grout in the shower gleams brilliant white. The floorboards are newly polished to a high shine and every room has a stereo so we can bring our own CDs and not have to body-slide to generic massage parlour music.

It's not all that busy, unfortunately, as it's brand new and nobody knows it exists, but I like helping Aubrey out and the few clients who come through give me a bit of cash. It's very close to the city and the men who come in usually do so on their lunch breaks, so there's a quick burst of clients after midday that pay the bills. I play Blondie on the stereo as I rub myself over these men, humming along.

The staff lounge is the terrace's kitchen, with a big glass sliding door looking out over a bare courtyard. There's usually just two of us on shift, and today it's a dirty blonde called

Megan. She's slender and petite, with a button nose and a few stretch marks on her belly from the baby she had six months ago. She looks young. *Really* young.

'How old are you?' I ask.

'Can I tell you a secret? Promise you won't tell Aubrey?'

I nod. Aubrey is upstairs with a regular client. I can hear the shower going, so the booking is almost over, but I haven't heard the squeak of her coming down the stairs just yet. I'm minding the phones, describing myself and Megan to the punters and I'm primed to answer the door if needs be.

'Sure,' I say.

'I'm seventeen,' she says. 'I stole my sister's ID.'

'Wow.' I don't know what I was expecting, but it wasn't this. I guess I was expecting her to tell me she was really thirty, and I could have exclaimed how good she looked. But what do I do with *this* information? I'm a bit speechless, but I finally get my bearings. 'How long have you been working?'

'A year. I started when I was sixteen, just before I got pregnant. Was doing full service at Strikers.'

Strikers is a very, very upmarket brothel. Lots of women from the industry have flocked there because it is exclusive, expensive and they can make some killer cash in a very short time. I don't know how her fake ID passed under the noses of the management of Strikers, it must be an extremely good likeness.

'Wow,' I say again, not really knowing what else to say.

'Don't tell Aubrey,' she says again.

I nod. 'Promise,' I say.

* * *

One night, my ex Will and I topple into each other at a trashy club where I've spent the night cutting up lines in the bathroom and buying mysterious pills off strangers. We always find each other.

We stumble back to his friend's house, sit in the garden smoking cigarettes and touching gently until someone comes home to let us in. Will is a former teenage problem drinker working on becoming a regular old problem drinker. I accept his drinking, he joins me in my drug use; we try not to wonder what the hell is going to become of us, and we lose ourselves in each other's bodies.

Will is a comfort, like home, a tie to a simpler time when all that mattered was that the bottle was half-full, we had most of a deck of smokes, and the night was still young. The curves and twists of his body are familiar under my fingers when nothing else makes sense. He knows my body so well, how to haul it up to the peaks and drop it down into the valleys. His bright blue eyes can peer into mine and it doesn't make me want to shrink.

I love him.

(*Or do I?*)

And I tell him so. I don't need anything else from him. He sees me. He sees who I am and accepts it, all of it. The effervescence I'm trying to kill but can't.

One night he meets me at Indulge so he can come over after work, but it's 3 am, the shift doesn't finish until four and the receptionists won't let me leave early. I try to convince them to let Will come in and hang in the staff lounge, but this is met with a strong no. Will is drunk, as he often is, and he flops around on the benches outside on the street. We yell to each other, me a storey up, hanging out the window, and him sprawled on the bench, skolling from a longneck, then casting the bottle off to smash in the gutter. When they finally let me leave, we make out in the cab on the way home, alienating and most likely titillating the driver.

I introduce Will to Amie, my two loves, and I watch them fold together, then turn their dual affection onto me. It is exactly as much attention as I need. We spend days in a druggy haze, fucking, the three of us. Will's slim body draped in silk and lace and rope, he's sweet and beautiful, distilled down to pure essence. I don't know if these feelings I have are real (*I mean, is anything even real?*) or just a transference of the sweetness of our early days through time. Either way, I bask in him, soaking up every drop of love and lust and joy that I can.

'He's so special,' Amie whispers, nuzzling my ear as we all

ignore the chaos of the drugs and try to sleep. 'Thank you for sharing him with me.'


Will watches intently as Amie hunts my arm for a vein.

'I don't know if you want to see this,' I tell him. I'm a little rinsed through with shame about it, but not enough to stop. Amie feels at the hollow of my elbow for the pulse, the right place to find that little doorway in.

'Nah, I wanna watch,' he says.

I do not want to watch. I never watch it happen; I always look directly away from whichever arm the needle plunges into. I inject drugs hundreds of times and I never once do it myself.

I don't want to know how to do this to myself because if I do, I know I won't ever, ever stop.

Anyway, I am the worst junkie. My veins are bastards. Slippery, thin, hard to find. Only the most experienced and persistent doctors can find them (and by that, I mean both actual doctors and the kinds of 'doctors' who specialise in helping other people shoot up). I spend so many nights, and afternoons and mornings, my arm extended, wrapped tight in the tourniquet as Amie digs around in the crook of my elbow trying to hit a vein that refuses to cooperate. I cry, bargain, and then dejectedly shoot the contents of the syringe, hot and tinged with my own blood, into my mouth because I know I can't get another vein.

I asked Amie to shoot me up in the early days of our relationship. She was hesitant at first, but I *wanted* it. It was my choice, my action, she just made sure I didn't try it myself and fuck it up. I don't do it every day. Every few days, at most. And I never try heroin, because I know exactly what I'm like. I can't even quit the non-addictive drugs. I've got a self-destructive streak, not a fucking *death wish*. We shoot speed, instead.

I have no shame. I ask her to shoot me up in front of friends, when I'm already drugged out of my mind, when we've been going at it for days and my veins are collapsed and sad. I fucking love shooting up.

When you look at any addict and wonder, *Why? How could they use a needle?*, you've gotta remember that it feels really, really fucking good.

I never maintain a constant habit. I go in cycles of four or so days where I do all the drugs in a well thought-out sequence, not all intravenously. Hit of speed, microdot, snort some ketamine, repeat.

I wear long-sleeved mesh tops to work when I have fresh punctures or bruising, trusting that the soft parlour lighting will hide the marks when my clothes come off. The first time I got shot up, when I was eighteen and fresh as a daisy, the 'doctor' missed my notoriously awful veins and I ended up with bruising from wrist to elbow. That this did not deter me says a lot about the kind of person I am. I would not jump out of a plane, *fuck no*, or go on a rollercoaster, but jabbing a needle filled with amphetamines into my arm? That is an acceptable risk.

This has nothing to do with Amie. She's just the delivery system. I've been waiting for someone who could do this for me. I've been waiting for it since the first time I tried a needle. Even when I wasn't thinking about it, the idea glowed gentle in the back of my mind like embers. Whenever I stumbled upon needles discarded in the back alleys of my suburb, something sparked in me at the sight of them, something hot and exciting flowed through me as I stepped around them. It made me remember the sharp pinch at the crook of my elbow, the warm flow of something mixing up with my blood and whooshing off around the rest of my body. I want it, I want it, I want it.

When Amie finally finds the vein, I let out a long breath as the hot curls of speed flow into my bloodstream. I feel my eyes sparkle, my heart pound, and the thing inside me that always feels hollow starts to fill.

'Wow,' Will says. There's something in his eyes.

Not disappointment. Fear, maybe.


Picture this: I'm clad in head-to-toe black plastic (all borrowed from Amie) and I'm at the mirror, painting my mouth a bright slash of red with my favourite lipstick: Revlon's Wine with Everything. It's the fucking best – great colour, nice and creamy, which is perfect if your lips are always dry, like mine. There's a tiny fresh hole in the ditch of my arm and my eyes glitter as my jaw works, tightening and clenching. Amie brings a CD case up to me and I kiss her, then do a tiny line of K. She's wearing a PVC catsuit, bright red, her hair in two buns on top of her head. We're headed to a monthly kink club in the city, and we take a cab because we're carrying so many drugs. It's not a good idea to risk public transport with drugs now that the cops are always patrolling with their accompanying labradors. ACAB, am I right? Even dog cops are bastards.

Everybody looks when we walk into the club, and it sends a gleeful spike of satisfaction through me. I immediately take my top off, garnering all the attention I need, and more. The night tumbles into a dream, a movie, as the drugs churn through my system. The club is small and packed, people pressing into me, hot like fever. Our sweat mingles. Suddenly I'm tied to a cross, and Amie is whipping my back with a heavy suede flogger. I can barely feel it except for the dull resonance of impact, the hits that throw my body forward.

People press in around, watching us, their eyes all glimmer and lust.

*I've never loved anything like I love attention.*

Amie grabs me by the hair and kisses me.

*I've never loved anyone like I love her.*

*(Or do I?)*

Then we're dancing, and a show is happening on the stage. A deliciously tattooed and slender young man swallows swords for our amusement. He is perfect, a madcap circus freak, and I want him. No, I *need* him. I tell this to Amie over the heart-slamming thump of the music. Later on, she finds him and tells him. I don't have words at this point. I'm all embodied, sweat and light. He kisses me, she kisses me.

The three of us are suddenly in the cold shock of night, then the lukewarm back of a cab, roiling hands and threading tongues. There's a moment in Amie's lobby, underneath fluorescent lights, when everything looks real and ugly, but it's just a moment and then we're in the warm womb of her apartment. The light swims, swims.

If you ever get the chance to fuck a circus performer while on a lot of ketamine, I'd take it. It is marvellous.

Picture this: the three of us, all unzipped, skin pressing on skin. Fingers dip and curl. My body reaches critical mass, becomes more than itself. I come so hard I forget where I am. I could be anywhere. I am everywhere.

And upstairs the neighbour beats on the floor with a broom handle, futile, trying to get us to shut up so she can sleep.

Amie looks at me through bloodshot, exasperated eyes.

'You need to leave,' she says. 'I think we both need to be alone.'

In our drug cycle, I exist in two states: high or coming down.

High is just fine. I love being high. Whatever the drug, being wasted is so much better than not being wasted. The sweet fog of weed; the jangle of speed; the giggle of acid; the slow, not-quite-there-ness of ketamine; the many shouted opinions of cocaine; the lovey, highly sexed feelings of MDMA. Four days of the week – Thursday, Friday, Saturday, Sunday – I am usually off my face.

I float or take off, watch the walls swirl with hallucinatory patterns. I laugh and laugh. I eat the inside of my mouth off on cocaine, sucking at the place where my nose meets my throat until it's raw, yell my exemplary opinions to anyone who'll listen until I'm hoarse. On enough speed I scrub the walls until they gleam, or vacuum for hours. Once, Amie and I crawl down the hallway of a friend's house on too much K and fall asleep in the dog's bed. With mushrooms the world smooths, becomes flecked with iridescent green dots and I feel more at peace than I've ever felt. After I smoke some particularly strong, purple-haired weed in a park, my friend's tongue comes out of his mouth, grows massive, and starts to boil.

I must pay for my excesses though, and I do not come down gently. I crash with terminal velocity. I cry hysterically for hours, sobbing until my eyes swell closed. The comedown from acid turns me into a crabby wreck; the after-effect of ketamine is a deep scraping at my soul. Enough speed will send me into a spiral. Ecstasy and MDMA are the worst: it isn't a comedown unless I want to kill myself. The price for each of these drugs is a deep low, and I combine my drugs profusely, so the cost is compounded.

'You need to go home now, please,' Amie says.

I don't blame her: even I don't want to be around myself when I'm in this state. I hide behind my sunglasses on the train home, weeping gently. When I get there, I burrow into my bed, sniffling into my blankets. I writhe and scream silently and rake my fingernails up my thighs. I hate myself with passion and fury. I think of my fourth-floor window, and I wonder if I should throw it open, tear off the screen, fling myself out of it. Will it be high enough? Will I just end up broken and battered? Would that be enough?

Why do I do this when I know what the cost will be? I don't know. I guess it feels like a decent price to pay.

Even when I'm having a terrible time on drugs, it's still better than being myself. The first time I do nangs, I inhale the nitrous oxide and slide down into the feeling. The world slips away to grey then black while my head *whomps*, echoing through my ears. I wallow there, low and open-mouthed, my eyes rolled back. There's fear here. *This is too much, too much.* When I come back up, I swear to myself that I'm not going to do it again, but when the cream bottle comes back around the circle to me, I slam that whip-it like nothing bad happened five minutes ago.

I simply cannot help myself. I'll do anything to escape myself, even if it means I'm scared, or I lose my mind in the after.

It's worth the pain to not be me.

Taking shifts at a new place, Bella, is like coming home. There I find women from Indulge, Slide and Exclusive, plus a few of the other places I've worked. It's a big erotic massage reunion! We party.

Bella is an old townhouse converted into a brand-new massage parlour. It has beautifully appointed rooms all the way up to the attic, and a sprawling girls' room downstairs. The rooms are minimalist and classy, done in shades of black and red with shining wooden floors. It's a dress parlour, so I drag out my old staples: the black one that makes my boobs look great and hitches up on one side to show my suspender and stocking top, even my old green flowered number for when I'm feeling like I want to be loose, braless and fancy-free.

Extras are A-okay at Bella, and it's close to the city, so I start raking in the cash. This is nice, as I've been in a bit of a lull with bookings drying up at Indulge and not much going on at Abernathy Street. I spend a lot of time at Bella sitting on men's faces and a lot of time at home counting my fifties. An ideal situation since my drug use has ramped up so violently – one needs a lot of money to stay so high.

I both love and hate the clientele at Bella.

Daytime means CBD worker dudes flood in on their lunch breaks, or earlier or later in the day for 'doctor's appointments'. These cubicle bros are neat, tidy and businesslike. They are often cashed up and smell good, like expensive aftershave and cologne. They want a break from their workaday lives, and I give that to them, in long, slow strokes up their backs; gentle, oiled caresses up their sides; slippery hands on their cocks. They don't quibble much about the extra prices and have nice crisp fifties for me, pulled from expensive leather wallets.

At night, though ...

Drunk dudes love a good massage. After a long night out on the piss they teeter in, swaying in the vision from the security cameras. They slur and stumble and catch their feet on the stairs as I take them up to the attic rooms. They can be overly loud, and it's hard to get them to relax. I've got to help them to the shower, make sure they don't crack their heads open on the tiles. Sometimes the massage itself gets too much for them. I'm working my way over some wobbly dude, body-sliding across his back, when he says, 'I don't feel so good.' I get him into the shower quickly, where he retches a little and spews up a thin stream of vomit that smells hot and sick like booze. Gross.

Drunk guys. Ugh.

Still, they pay my bills.

Andrew slicks a layer of silicone across my latex-clad arse, then sits back and grunts with satisfaction.

'Perfect,' he says.

The latex belongs to Andrew – he's got a massive collection of pieces in a huge selection of sizes. He has so much kinky equipment, and so many latex delights, that he has to keep it in a mid-size storage locker in a facility near his house. Earlier this evening we drove there, and Amie and I giggled as he loaded up his ute with boxes of leather, rubber, stainless steel, and high-heeled shoes.

Now we're high on ecstasy and each other, teetering around his flat in ridiculous shoes and head-to-toe latex. Amie, Andrew and I play weird games sometimes – a few weeks ago we did a whole bunch of ketamine, floated off into the atmosphere, and let him play with our pliant bodies. Andrew took good care of us, dressed and smoothed us with his hands. We came back down to ourselves, murmuring about how we felt like robot plastic dolls, movable mannequins that he posed and preened. All this is to say, we trust him.

I flex my feet in their absurd shoes, puff on my cigarette, and then an axe plunges into my head, cleaving it in two.

Okay, that's just what it feels like. There is no axe, this is a thunderclap headache. I pitch forward, screaming and grabbing at my hair.

'My head, my head!'

I'm in a black hole of pain, blind, and while I zoom

163

through the blacker than black, Amie and Andrew – who have no idea what is wrong with me – gather my useless body up, feed me some sedatives, and put me in the bathroom.

The cool tiles beckon; I slam my head into them over and over because it feels better than not doing it. The bathroom door closes, and the only light is a thin line under the door. I hear music outside, giggles. The sedatives take hold, curling up around my pain and, finally, I sleep.

I have a headache for the next week, but I don't visit the doctor. What would I say if they asked me why I didn't go to hospital? 'Yes, I thought I was going to die but I was also on drugs?' I don't know how to explain it. Later on, a doctor friend of mine says it could have been a small brain haemorrhage, a little spill of blood into my head that caused the pain, most likely brought on by the drugs. This staggers me.

Some of the trust is gone now. I trust Amie and Andrew to take care of me in a scene, maybe. But I no longer trust them to care for *me*. I had only dipped my toe into trust, but now I yank it out quickly as if it has turned ice cold.


'You should apply to the creative writing course at uni, muffin,' Amie says. She's just read a short story I've half-written. Amie is studying writing at university, and she tells me about the course, how it could help me to get better, gain more confidence with my words.

'Really?' I've followed the tales of Amie's adventures at uni, and I love hearing about what she's learning there, but university for me? I'm not sure. I'd applied when I left school, but I bombed my final tests and had only been offered my last choice, which I couldn't accept because I didn't have the cash to move out. Since then, I'd tried not to think about bettering my life, or even doing anything besides sliding towards the bottom. See, the reason I've not bothered to do much but go with the flow for the past few years is because I don't see a future for myself. When I imagine what will come to pass, there's a blank space there. Will I even last that long?

I do the application half-heartedly, because if I don't want it too much, it won't hurt if I don't get it.

I get a letter a few weeks later, asking me to come for an interview. I'm petrified. I tremble on the bus on the way in and ramble my way through the meeting, feeling small against the two professors who ask me gently about my favourite writers, and what I might want from the course.

'Margaret Atwood,' I say, trying to jam all my feelings into words that don't match. 'And Stephen King. Anaïs Nin. Poppy Z. Brite. Oh, and Carrie Fisher too.'

I don't know how to tell them that I can't stop writing, that it's the only thing I want to do. That it's the only thing I'm good at. That there's nothing I can imagine for my future, for myself, except that Amie thinks I could do this, so maybe I can. Maybe there's more for me than a black hole where my future should be?

It rains, heavy, as I walk home from the bus stop. I blink water out of my eyes.

*If I don't want it too much, it won't hurt if I don't get it.*

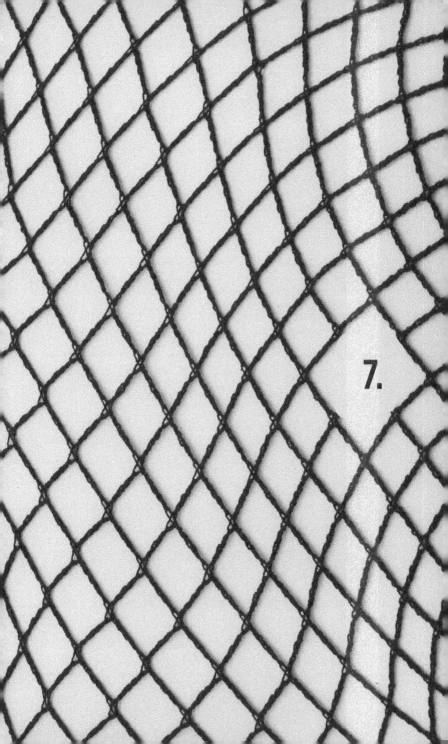

7.

I press the doorbell and hear muffled chimes inside. Amie worries at a chunk of her dark hair, twisting it up tight. I glance at the pedestrians fast-walking up the busy road. Do they know we're waiting to be let into one of Sydney's most well-known dungeons? Can they tell that just by looking at us?

The door opens and a lovely young woman in a simple black suit beckons us in.

'You're here for the interview?'

'Yes, thank you.'

She leads us into the waiting room, waves towards the couch and Amie and I perch on the edge of the chesterfield. We wait. I fidget, breaking out in pinprick sweat. From upstairs I can hear the rhythmic slap of a cupped hand on bare flesh.

Eventually an older woman with a long spill of shockingly black hair comes in.

'What has brought you to The Manor?' She asks. 'What is your sex work experience, what is your BDSM experience?'

We must give the right answers because she hires us both, rosters us on together, and assigns us our first collection of shifts to begin in a few weeks' time.

To work as a Mistress at The Manor, we must undergo an apprenticeship. This can take anywhere from six months to a year, as fast as our skill sets develop. In the beginning, we can only do the lightest of sessions – a quick spanking, some basic bondage, etc. As our experience grows, so will our ability to do heavier and heavier sessions, until one day we are given the title of full Mistress. I can't fucking wait. I see visions of myself wielding a whip, done up in shiny black.

Amie and I celebrate by going shopping. Our whoredrobe consists of the kind of stuff acceptable in massage parlours and brothels, but not suited to the dungeon. I've already got my first corset, a satin underbust number that I can lace to a moderate degree. To match this, we buy stockings (fishnet and sheer), new bras in black lace, shiny panties, suspenders and boy shorts. From a stripper shop in the Cross I spend far too much money on a pair of fetishy, black, knee-high PVC boots. The heel on them is spiky, high and dangerous. For me, the dress-up is half the fun. It helps me get in character. I don't identify as a lifestyle dominant, like a lot of Mistresses do. Nor am I completely submissive. Really, I'm more of a switch: someone who does both. I never settle,

I have to leave my options open. I like BDSM because it's fun, not because I'm compelled by any strong forces towards it, or because I gravitate to one extreme or the other. So, the outfits help me feel toppy, like a real Mistress.

I've got the costume, I can play the part.

'Come to the mountains,' Will says. 'Take a break from Sydney.'

His mother lives in the bush and he invites Amie and me up there for a week before we start at The Manor. I'm aching for a repeat of the few days we spent together – maybe this time we'll spend the whole week in bed!

I have no idea how I'm going to cope without a shitload of drugs, so I bring a bunch of weed with me, smuggling the mother lode nervously in my bag on the train. When Will's mother sees the half ounce I've bought along, she sighs and says, 'Oh, Mia.'

Oh, Mia indeed.

As Will and I career down dirt roads and into town to the liquor shop, my phone picks up a momentary signal and tings with a message from Amie.

*Hey Mia. I know I said I would come up after work this weekend, but I think I should stay home. Have a nice time with Will! I'll see you when you get back.*

Why did she even say she would come? I think that maybe

she's granting me some time alone with Will, but what I am yet to realise is that she likely wants an escape from me and my endless chaos, the sharp rise and dip of my mood during the drug cycle. I can't blame her. I want a break from it too, that's why I've come to this refuge in the forest. It's the first time I've taken a week off work in years.

Will and I spend the time playing with the dogs, smoking in the lounge room, listening to music and, of course, fucking each other senseless.

It feels ... calm? Like a reprieve from life, from work, from chaos. From the endless tilt and whirl of drugs, the nights spent digging around in the crook of my elbow. Sure, I'm still stoned as all that, but cannabis is barely a drug, is it? Without the swallowing of pills and sucking on acid, popping speed into my veins, I feel serene. I didn't know I *could* feel serene, I thought the only feelings that existed inside me without drugs were self-loathing and rage.

The morning air up in the hills is cool and pure. I wake up early, unfold myself from Will, and pad out onto the deck. I smoke as the sun rises, as light spills across the hills and valleys of eucalypts. When my feet get too cold, I butt out my cigarette, creep back inside and wriggle into bed with Will, hooking myself into his arms. He smiles his rare and dazzling smile at me before he goes back to sleep. I feel as though I could be anybody, living my life quietly, with a person who I love purely and simply.

*(Or do I?)*

And I don't hate myself here. I get the taste of that in my mouth.

All my belongings fit into a Toyota HiAce, with room to spare. Something about that makes me feel gloomy, and my bad mood echoes through the empty space in the van.

The drive to Amie's place feels longer with everything I own packed in tight behind me. With every corner we take, something clatters in the back of the van. I try not to jump with every bang and crash. I've got a weird, sick sense of doom in my gut and I try to ignore it, because it's moving day and I'm setting up house with the woman I love.

The first day, things go well. We celebrate.

On the second day, I'm coming down hard, right at the nadir of my ever-swinging substance parabola, sniffling into the pillows.

'Can you please sleep on the couch?' Amie says. It stings a little, this is my house too, but I acquiesce and curl up on the sofa, sobbing as gently and quietly as I can.

On my third day of living with Amie I hand the keys for my old apartment into the real estate. On the way home, Amie and I have a huge fight at the train station. The reasons why are dim, but it's worsened by the fact that I'm still coming down hard. I'm hysterical, nonsensical. I storm off, feeling betrayed and scared, dizzy from the after-effects of the drugs. I catch a later train home to Amie's place. My place. *Our place.*

Our other housemate comes out to meet me as I walk up the driveway.

'Amie says you need to leave,' she says.

'What do you mean?' I ask her, still walking towards the door, fumbling for my keys.

'You can't stay here any more. She doesn't want you here.'

'But ... I live here ...'

'You can't live here any more,' she says, placing a hand on my chest and stopping me from coming closer. I've just handed in the keys to my old apartment. I don't have anywhere to go. I tell her that.

'I don't know what to say, Mia. She doesn't want you here any more. You have to go.'

My head is spinning. It was just a fight, wasn't it? I can't see that it must have been the last straw. The comedowns, the drugs, the way I love Amie just a little bit too much, want to be with her every second, want to infiltrate every aspect of her life. I don't see that. All I can see is everything I hold precious falling away from me as I grab for it desperately. I start to cry there on the driveway, clutching at my handbag. Amie's flatmate heads back inside and I stand there for a while, trying to make sense of what's just happened.

Did we just break up? How can it be over just like that? Doesn't she know how much I love her, how much I need her?

I don't have anywhere else to go, and I've spent all my cash on drugs, so I can't call a cab or even catch the bus or the train. I keep crying and start to walk. I don't even know where I'm going. I walk down the highway towards the city for an hour or so, sobbing frantically, dialling every number in my phone that I can think of, leaving tearful messages on people's voicemails. No one is answering. It's not surprising. I've been such a drug-soaked mess that most of my friends are probably done with my shit. I've only got one or two left and they're not picking up. How dare they? When I need them! I call and call, hanging up every time I get the voicemail recording.

Finally, an acquaintance called Heather drives up beside me. She must have heard one of my hiccupping messages. I don't know how she found me, but I guess I'm hard to miss, stumbling down the footpath, weeping. She gathers me into her arms and puts me into her car.

'Where should I take you?' she asks me, gently.

'I don't know,' I tell her. 'I don't have anywhere to go.'


I mean, that was all totally dramatics, because I *do* have places to go, and my friend Jack's place is as good as any. He's one of the only people who has stuck by me through it all, put up with my endless and epic bullshit. He offers me the couch in his one-bedroom apartment. I take it and spend countless days on his sofa bed, scoffing valium and crying, wondering how it all fell apart so fast. Poor Jack, though, bless his heart, he puts up with my tears and benzo-ed demeanour, pushing the pills into my mouth in the hopes that they will stop me from sobbing. They don't.

Everything aches. I'd never had the kind of careening, agonising tumble of feelings for someone as I did for Amie, except maybe Will, and he's left town too, back to uni and his life and not me. I'm bereft. I ruined it. I loved Amie so much, I almost wanted to *be* her. That must have been a lot for her to deal with. With the clarity of being out of the drug cycle, I can see why she had to do what she did. I was a fucking wreck, even on my good days. I'm still a fucking wreck; it's just now I'm a wreck with a broken heart, and she doesn't have to put up with me any more. Fuck, I wish I didn't have to put up with me either.

I miss Amie so desperately it makes me want to vomit, to writhe and scream. I pop another of the little yellow pills, punch a few cones, wipe my nose and eyes raw with a tissue and add it to the pile by the sofa. Why can't the pills and weed kill my feelings? Why do I have to go through this, and how long is it going to take? I want every single pang to be muffled by the drugs. I want to feel nothing and be nothing and cease to exist.

Weeks pass. I leave the house only to go to work, where I make very little because I'm so sad, and to trip across the road to the 7-11 for smokes. I smoke until my throat is raw, my tongue blistered. I punch cone after cone, waiting to not feel terrible.

But it doesn't work.

Jack and I find an almost derelict old house to rent way out in the suburbs, and we move in so that he can have a life that's not taken up by a depressed girl on his couch all day. She has her very own room to be depressed in now! The place is actually crumbling, with holes in the floorboards underneath the carpet and water-damaged walls in half of the rooms, but it'll do. It's all I deserve, and all I can afford, anyway.

One day I *do* leave my new house, and I'm right by my old apartment. I take a quick detour over to the block to check the mailbox – I didn't have the wherewithal to redirect my mail. The box is stuffed with my post, no one has moved in yet. I shuffle through past-due bills and junk mail, until I get to one official-looking letter. It's been rain-soaked and dried again. It's from the university.

I open it with trembly hands and drop down onto the concrete, tears spilling out over my face, stinging my raw eyes. Everything goes quiet, dark, warps around the piece of paper in my hands.

I have been accepted to university.

The letter has been in the mailbox for a while. I have three days left to accept the offer.

\* \* \*

I've got a dim sense of fear and trepidation as I walk into The Manor for my first shift, but I try to stifle it as I ring the doorbell. At least Amie has rearranged her shifts so we don't have to be in the building at the same time.

The receptionist is an older woman called Lisa who greets me warmly. I instantly adore her. She shows me to the Mistresses' lounge, and I stand there nervously as the other women bustle around, getting ready for the shift.

'Hi, I'm Sasha,' I say from the door. They respond hello with disinterest and return to their makeup. I put my stuff onto the benches around the edge of the room.

'The seats are for the Mistresses,' one of the women tells me. 'Apprentices sit on the floor.'

'Oh, okay.' I put my stuff on the ground and try not to get in anyone's way. The mirror on the wall is full of Mistresses doing their makeup, so I take out a tiny mirror from my cosmetics bag and start to smear my face with gunk.

'Is that how you put your makeup on?' says a Mistress with a full head of curly hair.

'Um, yeah.' I puff out a nervous giggle.

She laughs. I'm not sure if she's laughing at me, or with me. 'I'm Hillary. So, what did you do before this?'

'Massage,' I tell her. 'I'm still doing it. And I'm about to start uni.'

She nods, brushing shadow expertly onto her eyes in front of a wall mirror. She's topless and I try not to look at her amazing breasts as she readies herself. I'm glad when she straps them into a leather bra, but they still look amazing cupped in the soft, black lambskin and I can't help but glance back and forth at them.

A fat white cat brushes past me. 'Ooh, kitty,' I say, and give it a scratch behind the ear.

'That's the house cat, Mistress Kitty,' Hillary says. 'She lives here.'

The cat becomes a good friend. I don't feel as though I have a lot of them here. I'm the youngest in the place by five or so years, and I don't have the wisdom or experience that other trainees might have. I'm not a lifestyler. I'm in it for the money and the fun. I'm not down to endure the kinds of power dynamic games the Mistresses play with the apprentices. My first act of defiance is to take a seat on the bench. There's a space behind the door to the Mistresses' lounge that no one sits in and I take this place, sitting lengthways along it behind the door, reading my books and trying not to bother anyone. It means I am out of the firing line, but it also means I go a little unnoticed.

Training is gleaned by watching sessions and getting lessons from the more experienced workers, but because I have such a weird manner and spend all day hiding in my secret seat, I don't get offered a lot of opportunities for practice. Still, I am taken into some sessions and slowly learn how to spank, paddle, flog, tie, cuff, role-play, penetrate and flagellate. I learn to mentally draw a box on someone's arse and aim perfect stripes in it with a cane. I relish the collection of skills. It feels like I'm filling myself up with something, like I've always needed to, but with something useful instead of wasteful. I take my job at The Manor seriously. I ease up on the valium. I do not smoke pot before work. I can see this is a great opportunity that I've been given, and I want to make a good impression, do a good job. I try not to be a fuck-up.

I try.

University starts before I even know it. One day I'm stumbling around the city, still mired in my pity party and pining for Amie, the next I'm at Orientation Week with a bunch of shiny and dimpled teenagers, learning how to be a student.

I don't know how this happened.

I mean, I do, and I don't.

How do I do uni? Like, how do I write an essay? I can't really remember. And how do I sign up for classes? Where are the classes? What classes do I take, what does 'critical thinking' mean, and also *how* do I 'think critically'? How does a person study? I have to figure these things out on my own.

The excitement of O Week is lost on me. I feel like a dark little storm cloud on the bright green campus. I blink against the sun and the brilliant blue sky, trying to follow the speaker as she tells us about the facilities, the student union, the uni bar. I sign up for classes in a fug, eyes darting all around the screen until I click a few random boxes and stumble out of the computer lab to smoke a cigarette.

My classes are populated by sweet young things with gleamy eyes and fresh notebooks, all pen-and-paper keen, jotting notes in neat cursive. My notes are barely legible half-sentences – I can't keep up. I forget what the lecturer says before I finish writing it. There are so many books to read: great, expensive piles of them that I buy with my dick-pulling money. I spill them across my floor and wonder how I'll ever read them all.

I peer around my fiction class from grey-circled eyes, spilling over with dread. It is the first time I've ever read any of my writing out loud, and it is terrifying. I dissociate, hard, as I read. When I'm done there's a debate about my story. This is called a 'workshop'. It is my turn to be ripped to pieces and it is vicious and thorough.

'You read your story in this flat monotone,' someone says, and the class nods. 'Like you're trying to be cool, or above it. Stop trying to pretend you don't care. You do. Stop trying to pretend you aren't scared. We all are.'

I mean, it's all so dramatic and bohemian, but he has a point. Jerk.

It hurts, and I'm scared. Not only to share my writing, but of the whole thing. I've swung from chaos into a place where I must be, or at least seem to be, together. It jars. I'm petrified.

How will I fuck this one up? I can't possibly get away with it, right? I'll never pull it off.

My classmates are all so fresh and new out of high school, eager and fucking beautiful and just teeming with potential.

I can never be that.

I'm watching for my connection, Unnamed Drug Dealer, at the front window when Isaac pulls up. He's early. I wouldn't say I'm *dating* Isaac – we're just sleeping together, but in a friendly and familiar way. He's a musician and a really nice guy. At least, he was at first.

Anyway, I have to watch by the window for the dealer because he doesn't come to the door. He doesn't even honk the car horn. He just pulls into the drive and waits a few minutes for me to come out. If I don't come out right away, he'll just drive off, I'll have to call him again and he'll be pissed with me.

He turns into the driveway behind Isaac and I race outside, fling him a hundred bucks for my quarter ounce, and give Isaac a wink as he gets out of his car, slipping the weed into my bra.

'What was that?' he asks as we head inside.

'Subterfuge,' I say.

He shakes his head. Isaac does *not* approve of my smoking habits.

And I don't know, suddenly I'm just not feeling it.

I tell Isaac this over the takeaway that he brings over, that maybe we shouldn't be fuck buddies any more, just friends, and we have a bit of a heated conversation about the whole thing. I can't understand why he's angry; we aren't together, he's mentioned multiple times that he's too busy for a relationship.

I don't know exactly why I'm over the thing we have going. Maybe it's the way he sweats profusely over my body when we fuck. Maybe it's the way I beg him to let me fall asleep first when he stays over because he snores so loudly that I can't sleep through it, but he never does, and I usually end up sleeping on the couch. Maybe it's that I secretly kinda want someone who *isn't* too busy for me.

'I don't need this,' he says as the fight reaches a peak. 'You're just a fucking whore.'

Boom. There it is again.

I can call myself a whore, that's fine. Other workers, yes: we can use it as a term of endearment. I love to tell my co-workers that I'm off to shower my 'filthy whore body' or talk about applying my 'whoreface'. But to have this man that I care for, in my own twisted way, use that word – it's like he's tearing a tiny strip off me. Something small, but important. He doesn't say it, he spits it. He's deliberately using that word to hurt me, and he has.

I don't know many men who are comfortable dating a sex

worker. I will say that they do exist – I have met them and seen a few workers involved with guys who really are well adjusted to the fact. Leo was okay with it, but Leo didn't really care about me. Jonathan hated it and used it against me. Will was okay with my work, but we weren't really together-together, and he's gone now anyway. Isaac said he was fine with it, but now he's gone and thrown up the 'whore' thing just to spite me.

'You were fine with me being a whore when we were fucking,' I say. He looks at me with disgust and storms out.

Fuck it. Maybe I won't date men any more, or just date other sex workers. Maybe I won't date anyone at all.

Then I won't have to explain a thing.

Hauling my sad arse across campus, I'm trying to decide if I should go to my next lecture, or just head right to the bar, when I spot Amie walking towards me. Things go a bit dark. My heart thrums double-time, and I choke back a surge of bile. Seeing her gives me a physical reaction, so dramatic is my woe. She gets closer and it feels as though my heart is down around my knees somewhere, glugging hard.

'Hi,' she says.

My moribund features are like a flashing sign – every emotion I'm feeling is writ massive across my face.

'Hi,' I say back, then mumble something about missing

her. I can't help it; the nonsense words flow out of my mouth without warning.

I can see it twist something inside her.

'I am sick of seeing your miserable face,' she hisses. 'I wish I'd never met you. Never speak to me again.'

The words thrum around my head as she walks away. I skip out on classes and take the train home, where I vent my pain in an epic, theatrical parade of self-mutilation. The show is for no one but myself, but I make it as dramatic as I can. I deserve this. I am awful, so fucking miserable that the woman I love wishes she had never met me. I wish I had never met me. For days I embark on this quest for blood, taking time out for classes (that I duck out of to burn myself with cigarettes and the red-hot tips of lighters) and shifts at Bella, where I make no attempt to hide my marks, and The Manor, where I do.

On the last day of my grand misery-fest, I hit my guy up for a gram of speed. I haven't touched the stuff since I broke up with Amie, but holy shit, have I thought about it. The way it feels, the hot curdling in my veins – it haunts me. Needles dance across my vision in dreams every night. I prepare the shot, doing all the parts perfectly. The needle gleams like a beacon in my hand, like a fucking holy relic. I tie off my arm and sink the bevelled tip into the ditch of my elbow. I get the vein, then lose it. Get it and lose it. Fucking slippery bastards! I can't afford to miss and be bruised for work at The Manor, but I want this, I need this so bad! I dig around in the crook of my arm for ages before I scream, the sound echoing through my empty house, and throw the needle across the room. I promptly chase after it and shoot the hot, bloody contents into my mouth (I'm not going to waste good drugs, hell no), then I collapse onto the floor and sob and sob. I'm mourning. For the needles. For Amie. For my whole life.

It is the very last time I ever have a needle in my arm for the purposes of drugs.

The next day I'm in a shiny white tutorial session room, looking around at the gleaming faces of my student cohort, and I decide.

That's it.

I'm going to be one of them.

I'm going to clean up. I need to do it, not just for uni, but for The Manor. I know that I can't maintain this level of fucked-uppedness and do a good job of either. So, no more drugs (I mean, no more except for weed, and maybe a couple of pills if it's a special occasion, and coke, well, if there's coke around then you'd be stupid not to take it …). But no more benders, no more four-day weekends lost in a drug cycle, no more surfing the internet in a K hole, and no more constant speed zings and crashes.

I'm a stubborn little thing. Just as I once made the decision to be high at all times, and followed that through to its horrible consequence, I now make the decision to stop. Once I have made up my mind, there's nothing in the world that can make me go against it.

So that's it. I stop.

It's over.


I need a new parlour close by my house. I'm so busy these days – what with uni and The Manor (where I'm not making much money, as I'm a brand-new apprentice and can only take the lightest of sessions) – that I can't haul arse over to Bella or Indulge for some quick money; they're just too far. I try a new tack: the suburban massage parlour. There's one not far from my place. I go for the interview and am hired immediately, of course. The place is labyrinth, studded with spa rooms down twists and turns of hallways. The waiting rooms are tiny boxes that fit an armchair and a worker's body for a meet, and nothing else. It is *busy*. It's got a name that no one uses: everyone calls it Hell.

I like to think of Hell as where erotic masseuses go to die.

At least, that's how I feel when I'm there.

The management and receptionists treat the workers with open hostility and disdain. They call us whores to our faces and act as if they're above us, even though our existence and deeds pay their wages. We workers, so many of us crammed on to a shift, sit in the lounge and watch Maury

Povich in the long slow hours of each day. The clientele is eclectic – tradesmen, older retired dudes, a lot of obvious drug dealers who bring in free product for us to share. Sure, I've 'quit' drugs, but everyone knows free drugs don't count. I consider myself practically sober now; I mean, I'm not high all the time. Except for the weed, I still smoke that at a stellar pace, but I'm abstaining from chemical drugs, most of the time. That's what sobriety is, isn't it?

Hell is where I get my first glimpse of ice, as girls cram into a backroom to hit the pipe, hiding it from the receptionists, who obviously hate it when the women smoke drugs at work.

'What is that?' I ask.

'Ice, fuckwit,' the blowsy, tough-looking woman says to me, blowing the chemical stink into my face. 'Want some?'

'Why not?' I say. Remember, free drugs don't count. I spend the next two days awake, and crying, and I never do ice again.

The place is an extras parlour, to the extreme, meaning that everything up to and including sex is on the table, all at competitive rates. When I quote my extra prices, the clients baulk, and try to haggle the prices down, quoting other workers' prices. I can't be sure if they're having me on or not. Jeez, I thought these were industry standards!

Despite the reduction in rates I make a fuckton of money at Hell, so I keep at it. Even when the receptionists call us all 'thieves' and 'cunts', even when the clients try to talk me down in price, even when my co-workers are whacked out on meth – I keep raking in the cash, so I keep at it.

It's worth it, right?

Right?

During my shifts at Hell, I meet a bevy of very interesting women. Everyone seems to hate working there, bitching constantly about the customers and especially the management, but everyone seems to have been there forever and they never seek brighter shores. The money is just *too* good.

There's Ellie, with the breast implants. She went from an A cup to a C with her first surgery but wanted to go bigger. The tissue around her implant hardened with the second surgery, capsular contracture, so she spends most of the shift when she's not in a booking massaging the stiff tissue, complaining at how she needs to spend twice as much as both initial surgeries to fix the damn thing. She makes me promise her I won't get implants, and I nod and promise, even though I was never planning to anyway.

Blue is the house Mistress, with a collection of whips, PVC and dildos. I pull her aside and tell her about The Manor, but she's not interested. She makes great money at Hell and she's happy, so I'm happy for her.

The twins are an odd pair. They are identical and don't

really mix much with us other workers. They whisper to each other in front of the TV and ignore everyone else. I don't think they do a single booking alone while I'm on shift with them. I'm fascinated by their stilted manner and curious at their paid encounters.

Bailey's mother drops her off at the front door for all her shifts and waits for her outside after. She's still in high school but she's eighteen, therefore totally legal, and she's cute as a button. She makes bank, so good for her.

Then there's Mandy. Mandy is a fragile flower, wilting in front of our eyes. She smokes a lot of ice, rarely sleeps, works constantly. She babbles often to me about the hideous things that have happened to her. I am scared of her at the same time that I am scared *for* her.

I give her my phone number for some reason, probably drug-related, and she calls me sometimes at 4 am, detailing stories from her past so horrible I really wish they weren't true. I believe her, though. There's something in the way she tells them.

'Mandy,' I say to her. 'you've got to get help.'

'Nah, love,' she says. 'I'm fine. Just had to get it out.' She hangs up and my phone goes *beep, beep, beep* and I cry until I fall asleep. There's nothing I can do to help Mandy. For years afterwards, until I change providers and get a new number, Mandy calls me in the early hours of the morning.

'Just had to get it out, love,' she says before she hangs up to leave me devastated for her in the dark hours of the morning. 'You always understand.'


I've never felt afraid in a booking before. I've got a good gut, remember? I've felt uncomfortable, disgusted, nervous. I've felt joyous, careless, and sexy as fuck, but I've not felt fear. Guys coming in mostly just want a good time, and I can pretend to be a good-time gal for an hour or so. There's a mutual trust there, an agreement that we're here for one thing: a sexy, fun time. I'm lucky.

I've never felt afraid in a booking before this one.

It starts in the usual way. In the meeting we discuss my service and the price for extras. He wants to go down on me as per usual and I'm like, *Sure. That's fine.* In the room he's a regular type, relaxing back into the table and breathing in hard as I tease my breasts around his cock. He flips me over, just a little too roughly, but it's fine, and he spreads my legs and begins to go down on me. Just a little too roughly. He's got serious stubble and after five or so minutes of gritting my teeth and bearing it, I say, 'You're going to have to be more gentle.'

He grunts, eases up for a second, then goes right back to grinding his sandpaper face into my cunt.

'Please ease up. You're hurting me.' It feels like every spiked hair is a tiny razorblade slicing me. I've got to save my vagina for other bookings today, but he's busy cheese-grating my vulva with his face.

He again eases for a moment or two, then goes right back to grinding those sharp follicles into my most sensitive of skins.

'Okay, that's it. You need to stop.' I slither out from underneath him, catching a glimpse of my raw pussy, aghast.

'I paid for it,' he snarls.

Oh. Here we go.

Even though I had to put up with a face-grinding down below for five or so minutes, even though it hurts me deep down in my guts, I take the money he gave me for my extras out of my little zippered bag and I hand it back to him.

'I'm sorry. It just hurts too much, your stubble is very sharp.' To defuse the situation, I run a playful and almost imperceptibly shaking hand down his chest. 'Let's finish, shall we?' I reach for his cock, but he slaps my hand away.

'I fuckin' paid for it,' he spits, and begins a tirade in this fashion as he dresses. He calls me a whore, a cunt. I don't know what to do or say. I just stand there, naked, as he rails at me. I can't remember where the panic button in this room is; is this enough to warrant it? His diatribe grows louder and more violent, and my frozen limbs flood with adrenaline. I grab a towel, wrap it around my oily body, open the door and run down the hallway towards the office.

He follows.

Now he's screaming at me.

When I get to the front desk the receptionists make a hasty retreat into the office. I go to follow them in, to escape from this man, who has grown huge and monstrous, vileness spewing from his anger-red face.

But they've locked it. They've locked the office door.

They've left me with this man, this red-faced rager, and now I'm really scared because it's just me, naked in a towel with a guy who is a foot taller and who outweighs me by fifty kilos at least. I don't know how I do it, but I turn around. I face him. I've got no choice. No one is going to save me but me.

'Get out,' I say. 'Leave, now.'

I don't know if he can hear me over his rant, and I am not sure where my strength comes from, but I start to push him towards the door.

'I want my fucking money back,' he screams, and I just start screaming right back.

'Get out! Get out, you fucking psychopath! Leave! Now!'

He gets this look in his eyes. I'm pretty sure he's going to hit me, but he strikes the wall by my head, making me jump, making me almost piss myself. Then he opens the door, walks out and slams it so hard the whole room shakes.

The lock to the office door clicks, then a crack appears. 'Is he gone?' the receptionist says.

I slump onto the floor and I start to cry.

The shakes start in the taxi on the way home. As soon as I walk in the door, I punch a few cones, gripping the bong with my trembly fingers, the lighter flickering with the motion. I punch more. I want to get so stoned that I forget the day and preferably my entire life. I pull cones until I can't feel my face, sucking up the hot smoke and blasting it out to make room for the next one.

In my mind I hear echoes of the sound his hand made when it hit the wall. I can still feel the way my bladder suddenly went loose, like my pelvic muscles gave up and fled the hallway, making everything inside feel like it was going to fall out.

I want to obliterate myself so I forget that feeling, never have to feel it again. Jack comes home from work and finds me incoherent on the couch. I mumble something about bad men and beard stubble that he doesn't question as he carries me off to bed.

Part of me thinks, *Well, it could have been worse*, and I know it could have. He could have not stopped when I asked him to. He could have hit me. He could have raped me. He could have killed me. Even though I've felt safe in my little sex-work bubble until now, sex work *is* dangerous. Sex workers worldwide are more likely to experience violence, especially in places where sex work is illegal. Decriminalisation makes sex work safer, and sex workers are more likely to report incidents to the police in states where the work is legal. The stigma surrounding sex work means that some people still think that doing sex work is an invitation to violence. *What did you expect?* This kind of socialisation is even in my own head. So, the funny thing is I only partially blame the guy. The rest of the blame I keep for myself. If only I'd put up with it, just closed my eyes and thought of fifty-dollar notes instead of getting him off me. If only I'd taken the day off work. If I hadn't started working at Hell, if I'd never started working in the sex industry at all ...

I know that it makes no sense, but I can't help feeling that while it *is* his fault for being an arsehole, it is just as much my fault for being a whore.

And this is wrong, so fucking wrong.


On my first shift back at The Manor, I'm perched above a submissive, doing a face-sitting session. I can't stop thinking about sandpaper stubble grinding on my tender bits, hands gripping my thighs too tight, his gruff grunts when I tried to stop him. Then I start thinking about being yelled at, chased, locked out ...

Fuck.

I don't want to do extras any more.

I used to love guys going down on me. As long as they let me do a health check of their mouth, peering in under a bright light for any signs of oral herpes or infection, I was open to all comers. I considered it a fucking happy bonus, and they *paid me*! Now some arsehole has spoiled it.

I stop offering it at The Manor, where it's known as 'pussy worship', and my income dives a little. Bloody hell, I absolutely hate that one bad client can spoil something I really enjoyed. Even in my personal life, oral sex is no longer the same. I've got cunnilingus PTSD. I fucking hate that man for making me feel unsafe with a face in my cunt. That's where I used to feel my best!

I don't even remember his name, so I can't curse it. I mean, it was probably Mark or Steve.

I develop a creeping distrust of my clients. I eye them differently now. Is that smile really a nasty grin? Does this one's gruffness hide rage? Is he going to switch over from taking a nice rub-down or a flogging to chasing me down the hallway at any second?

The specific and instant trust that must exist between worker and client gets harder to conjure and keep. I look at every client as though he might be about to verbally abuse me. And I have a deep distrust of the receptionists at Hell. I used to just hate them for calling us sluts and whores but now they put me in real danger. They didn't give half a shit about what happened to me.

All these transient customers; all strangers. How do I trust them?

How did I ever trust them?

It's no small thing to walk into a room with a stranger, undress and become intimate with them. It's like I'm only just seeing it now. Ninety-nine per cent of the time, it's fine and all that ensues is an oily, slippery, sexy massage time, or some good-natured torture.

It's not a one-way street either. A man also has to trust that the woman he is seeing will not do anything untoward, but it all comes back to that quote attributed to Margaret Atwood: 'Men are afraid that women will laugh at them. Women are afraid that men will kill them.'

The biggest risk to him is possibly that the sex worker might say something that he deems offensive, either generally or personally. She might massage poorly or hit a sore spot. The clients at The Manor have more to worry about, but we're nothing if not well-trained.

The biggest risk to sex workers? Death. Actual death. Then rape and bodily injury. I am lucky to avoid all this. I don't dare think of it as anything but sheer luck. One fellow worker told me that a client at a massage parlour offered her a fat line of what he said was coke, which she snorted. It turned out to be ketamine, and she went into a dissociative state and he raped her. That could have so easily been me. I'd have snarfed up that line in a second.

It's such a tenuous balance, this trust, and I don't know how to conjure it any more.

* * *

I make a few friends at uni, though I don't know what exactly they are drawn to. Is it my miserable face and demeanour, brought on by brushes with Amie on campus? Is it the highly inappropriate stories I tell about my life outside of classes?

'Hey Mia, how are you?'

'Tired. I didn't get home from work till four in the morning. And my arse is purple from getting caned last night. I can barely sit down.'

'Um, okay … Have you done the reading?'

I want to stop oversharing, but I can't. I'm no good at filtering; whatever I'm thinking about just tumbles out of my mouth. These kids are just out of high school, but they handle it with aplomb. I forget that I was just out of high school when I started working in massage.

So why do I feel so separate? Is this a case of me *being* weird, or me just *feeling* weird, and letting that alienate me from other people? I want what they have. Maybe through observing them, I can find the key. I've wondered how to be a 'normal person' as long as I can remember.

'What is normal, Mia?' one of my new friends, Emma, asks me as we sit on the back deck of the bar.

'I don't know. Normal is just … not this. Not crazy. Not a sex worker.'

'A lot of people are crazy. That's not something you can help. Put that aside,' she says. 'Do you like what you do? The work?'

'I'm not so sure about the massage,' I tell her.

'Quit then.'

'It's not that easy, though.'

'It kind of is,' she says. 'What about the rest of it?'

'Well, I really like working at The Manor. It's a lot of fun.'

'Then what's the problem?'

'It's just … not normal!'

'Why do you want to be normal so badly?'

'Because then I'd fit in with other people.'

She looks around the bar. All around us on the big picnic-bench seats, my new friends are chatting, drinking and smoking, and having a nice time. James comes back from the counter with a drink for me, puts it on the table and hands me my change. Peter rolls a smoke and passes it to me. Gillian chucks me a lighter before I even have to ask.

'I'd say that you *do* fit in with other people.'

Okay, Emma has a point.

Do I want to be normal, really? I don't know. Maybe it's just that I don't want to be a mess of a person any more. Maybe it's not that I want to be normal, it's that I want my life to be more manageable. I just want to feel better. So, I take the first step and I quit my job at Hell, and thus massage, all together.

8.

*T*hwack!

'That's for losing the McGrath file!' Norman says, then pulls his hand back for another swing.

'I'm sorry, sir!' I say, voice quavering, a tear welling and then rolling down my face. 'I won't do it again,' I promise him, but my attrition isn't enough. He draws back again and slaps my arse hard, right in the middle of the left cheek. The skin sings and the pain rinses through me. I am bent over a table, my hands tied behind my back, skirt raised, underwear and pantyhose in a puddle around my heels. I'm doing a boss–secretary role-play on the second floor of The Manor, door closed firmly and with the receptionist loading the washing machine downstairs. I am alone with this man and he is hurting me. When I arrived at The Manor for my Thursday shift and my only booking was a submissive session, I'd felt my stomach sink.

'Oh, Norman?' Marceline said. 'He's harmless. He's good fun. And good money.'

I'd bitten at the skin around my fingernails as I waited for the doorbell to chime, announcing his arrival, and when it did I almost jumped out of my little seat behind the door. He was an older gentleman, soft around the middle, with a kind face and a quiet voice that soothed me, somewhat.

In the room I'd let him gently chide me for my 'poor work ethic' and 'silly mistakes', let him tie my wrists, feeling cold trickles of doubt seep down my spine. But when he started to punish me, building up slow, warming my skin up like an old hand, I'd finally been able to relax.

*Thwack!*

'That's for forgetting to schedule my lunch with Steve from accounting!'

'I'm sorry, sir!'

I am not scared.

Norman doesn't want to hurt me. Well, he does, but only because *I* have okayed it. My enjoyment is part of what is making him so happy. I'm tied, stripped, vulnerable, having violence wrought upon me, and I feel as safe as I've ever felt. Norman does not make my gut shriek. His eyes don't blaze with anything except joy.

We work through his (reasonably unimaginative, rather sexist and patriarchal but otherwise harmless) fantasy, and as

I take the hits from the paddle and straps he wields, I feel as though I'm working through something else. It is aside from Norman, secret to him, but he's instrumental.

Being this vulnerable, and having that trust remain unviolated, helps.

After he's turned my arse bright red, marked here and there with deeper, darker bruising, and after he's worked himself into a state about it, coming in a tiny gush that he catches in a tissue, Norman unties me slowly. His face is flushed but he's beaming.

'That was wonderful! Thank you so much!'

I ease up, unlocking my knees and rising until we are face to face. When he sees the tear tracks down my face from my mascara, his eyes turn worried.

'Oh, I didn't hurt you, did I?'

'You did, Norman, and it was wonderful.'

After Norman, I start to see more dominant clients. I'm aching for that balm of unviolated trust. Good submissive sessions can be cathartic. They tear me up inside, sting and hurt, or are overwhelming, but when they're over I feel a deep serenity. The pain and mental turmoil bring me some relief from my usually roiling feelings. And the money! It helps, it really does. I learn there are all kinds of things I'll do for endorphins and the right amount of money.

I start to offer submissive tickle sessions, blocks of time where I am tied up and mercilessly tickled by a dominant client. I am incredibly ticklish, and my clients appreciate that I offer an unfeigned experience.

'I can tell when the girl is faking,' one of them tells me.

It's torture, all right, but I'll take it for the cash, and for what it gives me in return.

'Be careful,' I tell my tickle tops. 'I might thrash, kick you, wet myself … I'll definitely scream.' I do, I squeal the house down, especially when they find one of my *spots*.

Submissive sessions require a lot of mental preparation. Before the client arrives, I pace around, building myself up, half-excited, half-dreading what's to come. But during and afterwards, I have so much fun. It's incredibly satisfying to see the delight on my clients' faces, and it's like my own little secret when I take what I can get from it.

Sure, they aren't all great. Some guys *butcher* my arse with their inept spanking hands, tie me up sloppily, scratch me with their jagged nails as they tickle. But I *trust* them. I won't see a dominant client the house hasn't vetted, and I know I'm in hands that won't abuse my confidence.

It helps me to be okay again.


My bathtub is a deep chipped blue ceramic claw-foot number in a small bathroom off the kitchen. The bathroom looks like an afterthought, as though it's poised to fall off the side of our house with the slightest gust of wind. It has a black garbage bag up over the window, because when we'd moved in there was no curtain or rail, so we taped the plastic up and never got around to changing it.

A bulging piece of chipboard spans the tub, precarious. On it are the following: one pack of Benson & Hedges Smooth (one third full), an acid-green Bic lighter, an ashtray with two butts and one half-smoked joint in it, a notepad, a pen, a copy of *Madame* fucking *Bovary* that I have dog-eared six pages in, and my cat. She blinks down at me with her greeny-yellow eyes as I submerge halfway in the warm water and, as always, I try to keep her from falling in with the power of my thoughts. It must work, she never has.

I should be reading. I *have* to be reading. The essay is due on Monday and so far I haven't read more than half of the introduction, nor have I even made a .doc file. I pick up the book and open it again. The bath is my reading place. If I can't read here, I can't read anywhere. A moth flutters against the garbage-bag curtain, trapped between the window and the plastic. The noise zooms around my head. I wonder how I can explain a late essay to my tutor: *There was this moth, it was so loud I couldn't read.*

I try to fix my eyes on the page, but they slide over the words without taking any of them in. I go back to the top of the page and lock my eyes to the thick, blocky print. I'm ten words in when they unlock and careen around the page. I let my eyes go lazy, the letters bleeding out to grey static, then focus them again and try to pick up where I left off. Where did I leave off? My cat bats at the moth, catches it between her paws and eats it, wing dust in her whiskers.

*Concentrate! What the fuck is wrong with you?*

I chuck the book across the bathroom and the thwack of it against the wall sends my cat leaping off my makeshift bath-board, rocking the whole thing so that I'm almost showered with ash and butts, almost lose a pack of ciggies to the bathwater. I settle my equipment and turn on the hot water – the bath is getting lukewarm, I've been in it so long, trying to read this fucking book.

*I hate you, Flaubert. You are the cause of all my problems.*

He's not, though. I'm being too hard on Gustav. It's not his or his boring book's fault that I'm such a disaster.

Slipping under the surface, my ears fill with the sound of water splashing from the tap. I open my eyes and look up and out from underneath. The world swims above – edges of the tub, pale blue walls dripping condensation, the garbage-bag curtain, the fluorescent light that flickers just a tiny bit, just enough that I forget sometimes and think I'm getting a migraine. I need to breathe, but I don't.

*Maybe I just stay under here forever, which won't be much longer if I stay under here.*

My heart revs from standard thump to staccato pounding. The pressure builds in my lungs and blackness blooms along the edges of my vision. When the panic arrives, it rips through me like a current and seizes my body, lifting it up and out of the water as though a great hand is gripping me around the middle. I suck in air as my face cleaves the water, trying to breathe even though it's like my chest is being crushed.

Later on, I turn it into a joke. Everything's funny in retrospect.

'*Madame Bovary* almost killed me. But, like, for real.'

It's late one early autumn evening when Mistress Keiko pops her head out of the back door of The Manor. I'm sitting alone in the coolish air, smoking and trying to see the stars through the light pollution. My skin puckers into little goosebumps because I'm only wearing my work stuff (today a little red dress, fancy bra that pokes out of the top, stockings, suspenders, and boots – the little waist-cincher corset that goes over the top is folded up on the bench in my spot behind the door; it's too tight for sitting around in). Keiko gestures to me, so I stub out my butt and click-clack to the door.

'I've got a client who's happy to have an apprentice in,' she says. I'm instantly stunned, grateful and excited all at the same time. I'm being invited into a session for training! I follow Keiko around the dungeon as she collects a stock of equipment, piling it into my arms. Sounds (small metal rods of varying thicknesses that are lubed up and slid into the urethra), electric TENS units (for torture of the genitals), weights to be hung from tied-up balls; and lots and lots of dildos. I fumble all this stuff upstairs to the largest of the dungeons and set up everything for Keiko, doing my best to be helpful, then wait for them, nervously, fidgeting with a peg from a bowl of them by the door.

Edward is a regular. He doesn't have one Mistress he devotes his time and money to; he sees them all. His likes and preferences are set, and he requires the input of different Mistresses to keep it exciting for him.

There are no standard sessions at The Manor. Every booking is utterly unique. The combination of activities is always disparate, as is the order and tone. While different clients might all say, 'I want a session with CBT (cock and ball torture), corporal punishment and bondage,' the sessions will always be different. Maybe one customer likes a very strict Mistress to complete these tasks, and another likes a more playful tone. Maybe the levels of intensity vary. Perhaps one likes certain types of sensation, whereas the second likes different ones. Unlike massage, where there's a formula to the booking (rub, slide, tug, done) and the skill comes from how one interacts personally with the client, being a Dominatrix requires the capacity to be creative. A client might want all the things I mentioned above, and he might want them every time he comes in, but he doesn't want the session to be the same as the last one. Except for when they do – some clients have such specific fantasies that they recreate the same scenario every single time in order to satiate their desires. Mostly, clients are looking to conjure a specific feeling or sensation, and they vary their sessions so that the content is always different but produces the same results.

The necessity for creativity is part of what I learn as an apprentice, how to spin out certain activities in different ways, how to judge what kind of tone they like, how much they can take. It's why it is so important to watch a lot of sessions, to see how other Mistresses do it, to figure out what kind of Mistress I'm going to be.

Edward starts out his sessions with a bit of foot fetish. Keiko leaves this to me, so I unzip my boots, unhook my stockings and tease him with my feet.

I know what I'm doing here because I take a lot of foot-and-shoe fetish sessions. They are simple enough for an apprentice to do and not fuck up, so I've been doing them since day one. They mostly involve a lot of nuzzling, kissing and slobbering over my bare feet, or my high heels. I teach men to fellate my stilettos, taking the heels deep into their mouths, or to polish them with their tongues. They are easy sessions, where I spend most of my time seated, or stood above a naked man as he nibbles and sucks on my toes, or if he wants it, as I force my foot into his mouth, stretching his lips around the width of it. A plain foot fetish session can feel a little strained – there's only so many ways to instruct someone how I like to have my feet kissed, or the dirty soles of my shoes licked clean. When someone wants an hour-long foot-fetish session I die a little on the inside, racking my brain to think of ways to stretch it out. I learn to speak very slowly, move at half-speed. If a client has a shoe or boot fetish I gather as many as I can and spend the session getting him to slip them on and off my feet (some men *love* the sound a bare heel makes as it slips into a shoe). Once, I cover a client with shoes, hooking the high heels over his limbs, slinging boots over his chest. He comes in a shuddering shoe frenzy, gripping a pair of thigh-high leather boots in his shaking hands. I charge extra for foot jobs, because jerking someone off with my feet is *hell* on the thighs and core, and I'm not super fond of having to clean semen out from between my toes.

Edward just wants to suck on my toes, though, to fondle the arch of my foot and run his hands up and down my freshly shaven calves. Keiko gives me the signal that he's had enough time with my feet, so I instruct him on how to put my stockings back on and to slip my feet back into my high-heeled boots. He zips them up with reverence and we get him to stand. The foot stuff was a kind treat. Now Keiko is going to make him suffer for it.

I watch intently as she drags him through his penitence. I take notes with my eyes on all the ways she's just cruel enough for his specifications.

Being a professional Dominant is a weird thing. Sometimes

I don't feel very dominant at all. This is not to say that Pro-Dommes aren't actually Dominant. It's just that clients have their needs, their list of wants, sometimes even *scripts* that they expect you to learn.

'Charge him extra for that' is a common refrain when it comes to this kind of heavily controlled session (hell, it's a common refrain for everything). Sometimes the sub is *so* controlling that I wonder why I haven't made him pay my submissive fee instead of my Dominant one.

Edward isn't so bad, though. He suffers through a heavy bout of CBT with the weights, the TENS unit, the sounds, and even a few hearty kicks. He is rewarded once again at the end with the dildos, then Keiko wraps it all up with the standard hand-job. I take in everything: the way she plans and plots out the session, the way she moves and talks, how she carefully avoids cross-contamination, the way she watches the clock subtly and times out everything perfectly.

She's a craftswoman. An expert.

After he leaves, I glove up and clean the used dildos and lubey equipment. I'm in awe of Keiko. I'm in awe of all the Mistresses. They are so cool and poised and together, or they can fake it so well that I can't tell the difference. Fuck, I want that. Against them I feel small, a chaotic little fuck-up.

I just don't know if I can do what they do.

\* \* \*

For months, I'm all in pieces and I live two lives. They are very different lives.

I hold both realities in my head. I'm great at compartmentalisation. I take one life, put it in a box, and slip into the other. Of course, bits of it spill out, but nobody is perfect. My lives overlap. It'd be silly to expect there wouldn't be some overflow.

In one, I'm a student, rushing between classes, trying to study, writing essays at the last second, spending afternoons at the uni bar getting messy with my fellow students.

In the other, I'm high-heeled and clad in PVC, lips slashed with red, riding men like ponies through the halls of the dungeon; or clad in a school uniform and long white socks, bent over a desk, taking a spanking.

Both lives are great, but I am not. Why aren't I happy? I'm skipping between two paths that are objectively wonderful and that leave me room for progression – why isn't it enough? I don't have time to deal with my broken heart, my fractured brain, my fear, and the ache in my veins and bones for drugs to escape it all. I lock it down, put it in a box, vow to deal with it later.

I spread myself thin across my lives, and everything I've boxed up spills over now and again. I have breakdowns at uni. I lock myself in the bathroom to hyperventilate at the dungeon. I stare at the blinking cursor as I work on one assignment or another, unable to think or lift a finger to type, or do anything but stare as the clock ticks and the due dates grow closer and closer. My marks are mediocre. I am half-arsing two things, instead of full-arsing one. I'm too divided in my multiple lives to give my full attention to one, yet both require it.

Uni and being a Dominatrix: they both *matter.* They matter to me. It's as though I've swum up through time from those days when I felt plastic. I don't feel like I'm not real any more. The things that I do are real things with real consequences for real people, including myself. These things, they matter. I *care.*

I know who I am now. I'm a fuck-up but I'm not a bad person. I'm a lovable disaster, a chaos whirlwind of a woman. And I'm kind of aware that there's something waiting for me up ahead, and who knows? It might even be good.

I just don't know if it's *this.*


I ask Jack what he thinks as we eat dinner.

'If I had to choose, which should I go with?'

He looks me full in the face, swallows his mouthful fast and says, 'University. No doubt.'

'Don't answer too quickly!' I laugh at him, as he coughs around the food caught in his throat. I smack him on the back as he wheezes.

'You can be a Mistress anytime,' he says when he recovers.

'This course is too important. I think studying is good for you.'

He is saying what I'm too scared to think. I don't want to give up being a Mistress! I love learning to be a Pro-Domme, and I love the money. If I were a different person, not so mixed up and all over the place, being a Mistress while I got my degree would be perfect. Good money, few hours, lots of time for studying. But I am the person that I am, messy and chaotic, and learning to be a Mistress, a *good* Mistress, requires more of me than I can give right now.

'Maybe you could go back in a couple years' time, when you're ... better,' Jack says. I know he means: when I've got my head on straight.

'I guess I can.'

'So, you're going to do it? You're going to quit?'

'Don't sound so excited!'

'I just want you to be happy,' he says.

'Me too,' I tell him.

I call the owner of The Manor and explain to her why I need to quit. I don't just walk out. I don't let my frustration allow me to act out and then get fired. I do not burn this bridge. I am a grown-up, for the first time ever, and I explain myself to someone else. She understands.

She leaves the door open for me.

Callie hands me the teapot and I put it on a saucer, atop the standard paper doily.

I fucking hate these doilies.

I spend at least thirty minutes per shift peeling them from the bricks they come in, then tipping them in the bin when I clear the tables. It sums up perfectly the kind of ridiculous busywork that comes with 'standard' jobs. I peel the doilies because they go under the teapots and the lattes. Why? Because they just do. The real reason is to give us something to do so that our boss doesn't feel like they're wasting the pissy wage they pay us per hour. Peel the doilies, throw them away. This kind of labour has never made sense to me.

I have to pay the bills, though.

I load the teapot into my already laden hands, then spin on my sneakered heel and take it over to table six. I put down their cappuccino first, then the teacup. As I go to put the teapot on the table I miss and spill the entire pot of boiling water all over my hands. I start to cry in the middle of the cafe.

Nobody gave a shit about the three-year gap in my résumé when I applied for hospitality jobs. The third cafe I went to asked me if I could work Saturdays, I said yes, and I was hired on the spot.

I'm a really good waitress. I'm fast, precise, and don't often fuck up. I make okay tips because all those years of acting as a sex worker taught me to be able to pretend that I'm a nice girl, and I can plaster a big smile on my face, chat and make jokes with the customers even though I'm exhausted.

On the inside though, I'm full of rage.

There's something about being on my feet all day that turns me furious. As I hand customers their stupid fucking lattes with a shit-eating grin, in my mind I'm imagining their fiery deaths. I'm picturing throwing flat whites right into their faces. My masked rage and infamous mood swings earn me a reputation at work. One of the baristas calls me 'Medea' and laughs when I gnash my teeth as I walk into the kitchen and slam orders down, swearing. They don't fire me, though, because I can switch the smile back on before I greet another horrific noisy family at the front and show them to their table.

I run the cold kitchen tap over my burnt hands for as long as I can. After five or so minutes the shift manager, Julio, appears at the door.

'We've got a table of eight waiting to order, are you done?'

Am I done being burned?

'Oh Julio, I am *so* done.'

But I plaster the smile back on, wipe my stinging hands on my apron and go back out onto the floor, all for the princely sum of twelve dollars an hour.


It hurts to hand the fifty-dollar note to Unnamed Drug Dealer as he idles in my driveway. It's a sharp jab into my brain, my heart and my wallet. There are so few of those fifties in my yellow envelope pay packet. Each one is so precious.

Under my new life regime, I'm forced to curb my cannabis usage massively, and this greatly improves a lot of things: my mental state (though only somewhat), my health, and my capacity to complete my university coursework. I cut down from what was oftentimes a half ounce per week, to a more sensible three grams – because that's all that I can afford.

In a deliberate display of catharsis, I take my bong, put it in a plastic bag and smash it with a hammer. I'm tired of being controlled by it, that punch in the face of cannabis and nicotine. I've spent years of my life in thrall to my bong, clutching it to my face like a dummy, bubbling smoke through the blackish water within. Smashing it is like banishing a lover I adore but know is not good for me. I cry as I bash the hammer into its sturdy form, feeling it splinter to pieces with every hit, feeling it in my blood.

Now, I roll tiny joints that I smoke with far less intensity than I pulled cones. It feels more valuable this way. It means so much more now that every dollar is so hard won, takes such a toll on my body. Not that sex work was easy money, just ... there was more of it. More money, far less physical strain. And I could call in for an extra shift if I was low on cash and needed drugs, but now my shifts are set in stone each week, my wage promised but meagre.

It's as though I've sabotaged my drug addiction by making

less money, a move that works out in my favour. I always knew that the glut of quick money from sex work enabled me.

Of course, it isn't as easy as all that. Curbed usage comes with many nights and afternoons and mornings spent rolling around on my bed, aching with need, the feeling tugging at my throat and lungs and brain and bone marrow. I run out and have to go *days* sober, the nights of which are usually spent crying myself to sleep.

When Unnamed Drug Dealer backs out of my driveway with a curt little wave, I go inside and divide the buds between two small zip-lock bags.

'Take this for me, will ya?' I ask Jack, handing him one of the bags. 'Don't let me have it until Thursday, no matter how many times I ask.'

'No offence, but can't you just control yourself?'

I am bewildered. Have we not met? 'Um, no?'

'Okay,' Jack says. 'But I'll hide it in my room. If you go in there and try to find it, you're gonna break the friendly trust and house-matey simpatico we've got going.'

'I wouldn't do that, which is why I'm giving it to you.'

'Yeah, going through someone's room? That's, like, real drug addict stuff.'

I look at him with raised eyebrows.

'Nah ... you know what I mean.'

\* \* \*

There, look, Mia, you have your 'normal' life. (Mostly) off drugs. Mainstream job. You are, once again, relatable. It's what you wanted, so how does it feel?

It feels pretty shitty, to be honest.

I kind of miss massage. I really miss being a Mistress. I miss the staff lounges and camaraderie, the big stacks of cash. I miss the good clients and the way every day was different. I miss fancy lingerie and PVC. I miss feeling like a sexy fucking bitch. I miss the way Lisa, the receptionist at The Manor, would make up songs about me and croon them when I was feeling down. I miss the gleeful, surging joy I'd get from a good corporal punishment session, giving or receiving. I miss John and his specific fantasy. I miss the *click-click-click* of heels across tile and the way that the women at work would be so open, so boundary-less, so real. I miss the good clients, the way I could bring a bit of whatever they were looking for into their lives for thirty to sixty minutes.

I don't miss the bad clients, the shitty management, or the bad days, bad weeks, bad months, money-wise.

I hate working in hospitality. My boss is an arsehole, he sexually harasses us and pays us illegally and terribly. I do long shifts with no breaks. I'm angry all the time, and my body aches so hard after shifts that I feel old and haggard, and I'm only twenty-two. But I work with some good people, kind and hard-working folk who are generous with what little they have, and they are still smiling and funny even though they spent their days busting their arse for jack shit.

As I reel around my new life, I know this is for the best. Not because there is anything inherently wrong with sex work. It's because I never used sex work well. I let it enable me to be a drug addict and to let my mental illness get out of control. If I was a different kind of person, sex work would have been a great way to get myself ahead. I liked the work, the atmosphere, and if I had been smarter, I could have saved some of the money I made. Used it to make things better. Instead, I let it crash and burn me.

Sure, my life is a lot more relatable to my peers and I feel like I'm not living in two worlds now. That is a nice feeling. But I'm still mentally ill, though without a firm diagnosis (and unaware that I'll wait over a decade for one). I'm still a ball of chaos and endless calamity, sex work or no. I just no longer have the money to feed that chaos, go deeper into it. And I no longer have the time to let it consume me. I've got classes to take, shifts at the cafe to do, assignments to complete.

It's been a long, long time since I heard from her, but one afternoon my phone beeps and I open the text.

*Want to meet for a coffee?*

*More than anything!* I text back.

It's from Zara.

We arrange to meet a few days later. I wait for her out the front of the cafe and jump with glee when I see her. As she comes towards me, I notice that there's something different about her body. She doesn't have the slim, svelte lines that I'm used to.

'Oh my god, you're having a baby?' I say as she hugs me, pressing the firm curve of her belly into mine, kissing me on both cheeks.

'Yes, can you believe it? It's a girl!'

'This is amazing! Can I touch?' She nods. I rub her stomach, plant my face on it and whisper to the baby girl inside, about how her mum is amazing, and how I can't wait to meet her. Zara laughs and we go inside and sit down.

I catch up on all the gossip. Zara is still working at Boutique, though she's switched over to reception while she's pregnant. She tells me about the women I remember, and all the new faces, the endless churn of workers through the door. We reminisce about our days at Slide, Calvin and Serena, the rails of speed and long nights in the girls' room. She's still dazzling, the aura of pure light that bursts from her is still as true as always. I tell her about the past few years: the careen around Sydney's parlours, the drugs, cleaning up (well, kind of), university, and The Manor.

'But I've quit,' I say. 'I've left the sex industry. I'm working in a cafe now. It sucks, but I think it was the right thing to do.'

'That's good. I always felt like ...'

'Like it enabled me?'

'Exactly. Maybe go back to working at The Manor when you've got your head on straight.'

'Right?'

'You'll get there,' she tells me. 'You're going to do so well at whatever you try.'

'Thank you.'

'What for?'

'I dunno. For seeing something in me worth saving.'

Epilogue

In the ensuing years, I do go back to sex work. I dip my toe in and out.

After uni is finished and I settle into a career, I make some quick extra cash now and again through sex work, on a needs-must basis. I meet a mysterious and fascinating woman who works as a Mistress and, for a year, I train and take sessions with her at her private dungeon, not even for the money but because I find the work fun. My day job is mindless, and I have the headspace to devote to learning the work of being a Dominatrix. She teaches me valuable lessons on safety, thoroughness, cleanliness and the psychology behind dominance and submission.

I find the perfect balance for me, which is doing sex work for fun and extra money while otherwise employed. The stress of having to depend on unreliable income doesn't factor in. When the Mistress moves states, I don't reach out to other dungeons. I pull my toe out of sex work again, dip it back in when the mood takes me.

Currently, I take sessions as a Pro-Domme once a week. It's my side hustle. It's great fun. I wish I could tell people how much fun I have. I can't though. The stigma is real. It doesn't matter how much I feel as though what I'm doing is right for me, and makes me happy, there will always be people who just don't fucking get it, think that it's immoral. Think there's something wrong with what I do or who I am. I'm a grown woman of sound (or sound-ish) mind, with two fulfilling and successful careers who makes the choice every day to do what I want to do.

I guess I just don't want to fulfil the standard narrative of sex work being something negative. For some it is, for me it wasn't, aside from the fact that I let it enable my drug addiction and the great zigs and epic zags of my moods. I never felt like anything I was doing was wrong. Outside of the mainstream, yes. But never wrong. And I still don't. I read recently that there are approximately twenty thousand people working in the sex industry at any one time in Australia. If you think you don't know someone who has done or is doing sex work, you are most likely mistaken.

Some people who choose the profession don't have many choices, but I did. I have privilege – I'm white, educated, able-bodied, and from a first-world country where sex work is legal – and I had the ability to choose it. I did choose it.

I thought that the way I've always wanted *more* in my life meant more drugs, more sex, more dramatics, more chaos. I thought it meant I did not want to live a safe life. But what it really means is that I don't want to live a rote life. I don't want to live dispassionately. There are ways I can achieve this without doing damage to myself. The freedom I felt when I left home, to live any kind of life I wanted, to me no longer means that I can and should lose control. The 'normal' life I thought I wanted? I never wanted that. I just wanted better for myself than a constant chase for drugs and drama.

I can live an extraordinary life without hurting myself.

# ACKNOWLEDGEMENTS

Thank you to my first readers: Savannah Neptune, Lauren Ingram, Alison Evans, Rabia Azad, Meg Elison, Anna Westbrook, and Maddison Stoff.

My dearest thanks to the people at Echo, then and now: Angela Meyer, Liz Robinson-Griffith, Tegan Morrison, Benny Aigus and James Elms. Special thanks to my publicist, Brendan Fredericks.

My deepest appreciation to Corey for his painstaking edit of a book full of all the most hectic and filthy stuff I've ever done.

Thanks to the real 'Renee', 'Will', and 'Jack' for all the stuff we went through, and then letting me write about it many years later.

Thank you to 'Amie', for helping me to this path. I, too, wish we had met as adults; not the scared, raw kids that we were.

Lastly, thanks to 'Zara'. Your support is part of the reason I made it. Thanks for always seeing the best in me.